Y0-BDA-565

CONTENTS

NEW DIRECTIONS FOR TEACHING AND LEARNING

Marilla D. Svinicki, *University of Texas, Austin*
EDITOR-IN-CHIEF

R. Eugene Rice, *American Association for Higher Education*
CONSULTING EDITOR

Technology: Taking the Distance out of Learning

Margit Misangyi Watts
University of Hawaii at Manoa

EDITOR

WITHDRAWN
WRIGHT STATE UNIVERSITY LIBRARIES

Number 94, Summer 2003

JOSSEY-BASS
San Francisco

LC
5803
.T4
T42
2003

TECHNOLOGY: TAKING THE DISTANCE OUT OF LEARNING
Margit Misangyi Watts (ed.)
New Directions for Teaching and Learning, no. 94
Marilla D. Svinicki, Editor-in-Chief
R. Eugene Rice, Consulting Editor

Copyright © 2003 Wiley Periodicals, Inc., A Wiley Company. All rights reserved. No part of this publication may be reproduced, stored in a retrieval system, or transmitted in any form or by any means, electronic, mechanical, photocopying, recording, scanning, or otherwise, except as permitted under Sections 107 or 108 of the 1976 United States Copyright Act, without either the prior written permission of the Publisher or authorization through payment of the appropriate per-copy fee to the Copyright Clearance Center, 222 Rosewood Drive, Danvers, MA 01923, (978) 750-8400, fax (978) 750-4744. Requests to the Publisher for permission should be addressed to the Permissions Department, c/o John Wiley & Sons, Inc., 111 River St., Hoboken, NJ 07030; (201) 748-8789, fax (201) 748-6326, e-mail: permreq@wiley.com

Microfilm copies of issues and articles are available in 16mm and 35mm, as well as microfiche in 105mm, through University Microfilms Inc., 300 North Zeeb Road, Ann Arbor, Michigan 48106-1346.

ISSN 0271-0633   electronic ISSN 1536-0768

NEW DIRECTIONS FOR TEACHING AND LEARNING is part of The Jossey-Bass Higher and Adult Education Series and is published quarterly by Wiley Subscription Services, Inc., A Wiley Company, at Jossey-Bass, 989 Market Street, San Francisco, California 94103-1741. Periodicals postage paid at San Francisco, California, and at additional mailing offices. Postmaster: Send address changes to New Directions for Teaching and Learning, Jossey-Bass, 989 Market Street, San Francisco, California 94103-1741.

New Directions for Teaching and Learning is indexed in College Student Personnel Abstracts, Contents Pages in Education, and Current Index to Journals in Education (ERIC).

SUBSCRIPTIONS cost $70 for individuals and $145 for institutions, agencies, and libraries. Prices subject to change.

EDITORIAL CORRESPONDENCE should be sent to the editor-in-chief, Marilla D. Svinicki, The Center for Teaching Effectiveness, University of Texas at Austin, Main Building 2200, Austin, TX 78712-1111.

Cover photograph by Richard Blair/Color & Light © 1990.

www.josseybass.com

FROM THE SERIES EDITOR

About This Publication. Since 1980, *New Directions for Teaching and Learning (NDTL)* has brought a unique blend of theory, research, and practice to leaders in postsecondary education. We strive not only for solid substance but also for timeliness, compactness, and accessibility.

This series has the following goals:

- To inform about current and future directions in teaching and learning in postsecondary education
- To illuminate the context that shapes those new directions
- To illustrate new directions through examples from real settings
- To propose how new directions can be incorporated into still other settings

This publication reflects the view that teaching deserves respect as a high form of scholarship. We believe that significant scholarship is done not only by the researcher who reports results of empirical investigations but also by the practitioner who shares with others disciplined reflections about teaching. Contributors to *NDTL* approach questions of teaching and learning as seriously as they approach substantive questions in their own disciplines, dealing not only with pedagogical issues but also with the intellectual and social context out of which those issues arise. Authors deal with theory and research, and with practice, they translate from research and theory to practice and back again.

About This Issue. In this issue we take a slightly different approach to the topic than is customary. To the regular chapters on philosophy and pragmatics the issue editor has added two interviews with individuals outside the field of higher education, but within the field of technological advances. By bringing in the insights of these nonacademics, she hopes to help us understand the perspectives of the world that shapes our institutions and the futures of our students.

Marilla D. Svinicki
Editor-in-Chief

MARILLA D. SVINICKI is director of the Center for Teaching Effectiveness at the University of Texas at Austin.

EDITOR'S NOTES

> A new technology does not add or subtract something. It changes
> everything.
>
> —Neil Postman

One of the main questions that lingers in the halls of academe is, Why should we include distance or distributed learning modalities in the delivery of education? The term *distance education* itself is problematic in that it encompasses a wide range of technologies as well as possibilities—from master's degree programs to corporate and military training. Certainly, the new communication technologies have changed both traditional and non-traditional venues. For instance, commuter schools are offering more and more online and video courses, special programs, and degrees, using the new technologies that can be found at most colleges and universities. Outreach arms of colleges and universities use varying technological modalities to extend their reach, especially for continuing education purposes, and regular departmental offerings now include online options for taking courses. There has also been a growth of for-profit entities such as the University of Phoenix, corporate universities such as Motorola, and universities such as Jones-International and Harcourt University, which are primarily online. These all cater to a growing number in the population who are looking for flexible educational opportunities, as well as those who are closely aligned with their employment needs.

A small percentage of the students buying into this new modality of teaching and learning are eighteen- to twenty-year-olds, as well as working professionals, people completing a degree, older students interested in learning but not necessarily wanting to obtain a degree, and people looking to acquire new skills. In 2002, there were over two million people taking online courses. The University of Phoenix alone has reached over ten thousand students a year and it hopes to reach two hundred thousand in the next decade.

The kinds of technologies used for distance learning are varied; they are television, two-way video, the Internet and the World Wide Web, satellite delivery, virtual communities, videotapes, and a combination of any of these applications. The choice about which application to use is often based on pedagogical issues, is sometimes based on cost issues on both the sender and the receiver end, and is often based on the comfort level of those using the system. Thus, you have faculty who are delighted with video conferencing and others who eschew it. You can find faculty who swear by the software application called Blackboard, and there are others who would not trade WebCT for a new model. Thus, the technologies are personal and adaptable, provided they are affordable.

Three quarters of two- and four-year colleges offer distance learning opportunities at this time. A third of these offer accredited degree programs online. Some people predict that, soon, most colleges across the country will be offering some of their courses online and that by the year 2004, a hundred million Americans are expected to take part in continuing education, using some form of the new communication technologies.

As we've moved into a knowledge economy, work and learning have become one and the same. If we really think about what lifelong learning means, we can see that it is not connected to a physical space, such as a school or college. It is a flexible concept that is connected to life, which happens everywhere.

So why become part of this movement? There are many answers one might have to this question: everyone else is doing it, we need to get on board with the future, we can't lose students to other institutions, it might be revenue-producing, it sounds exciting and interesting, or it certainly seems to be on the cutting edge. However, people should perhaps not be so willing to climb on board this movement. Why not? It could be an overly hyped marketing concept, failure is easy—as has been proven by many a fallen endeavor, there is huge competition in this marketplace, there might be a conflict of interest between solid educational practice and the production of revenue, the supply will perhaps shortly outweigh the demand, buying into this is a financial strain on any institution, or it could be that the support services and infrastructure necessary to sustain any effort are huge.

The questions Why? and Why not? are not answered readily. Many in higher education are restating their mission and goals to include more flexible forms of educational delivery. At the same time, faculty members are questioning the efficacy of these new modalities in light of other issues facing higher education.

This volume suggests that for higher education to survive, as we know it, it must incorporate technology to broaden the delivery base for courses. However, we must be cognizant of the cost of doing so—the cost to the practice of teaching and learning as well as the cost of the technology itself.

Margit Misangyi Watts
Editor

MARGIT MISANGYI WATTS is director of Rainbow Advantage/Freshman Seminars at the University of Hawaii at Manoa. She is active in the national movement for information literacy, is involved in campus initiatives in distance learning, and recently wrote a text for first-year students, College: We Make the Road by Walking.

1

This volume addresses some of the implications of technologies for teaching and learning. Technology is viewed as a catalyst to improving educational practice.

Introduction: Technology as Catalyst

Margit Misangyi Watts

There is a current of frustration among many faculty members that is based on feeling pressured to produce distance education. Yet others suggest that there is no excuse to *not* use the new available tools. These educators find that using technology intelligently will almost certainly extend both reach and results. But those frustrated ones might agree that the reach is extended but aren't so certain about the results. Understanding that one of the goals of a liberal education is to openly debate and defend cultural assumptions, we need to perhaps come to terms with the explosion of technology that promises to change our educational paradigm. Faculty must view themselves as learners, along with students, using the new technologies together in an exploration and analysis of the world and its meaning.

This volume addresses the profound questions, and their implications, that stem from the tide of new technologies thrust into our lives. The narrative focuses on the educational arena, as it has become the emergent venue for conversations about technology. Rather than deal with specific instances of success or failure in classrooms, or contributing to theories about various applications of software and hardware, this issue addresses technology—specifically the new computer technologies—as a new cultural symbol. These chapters should encourage participation in meaningful conversations about technology in general and how it affects education in particular.

General Musings

For Marshall McLuhan, the medium was very much the message. However, with the new technologies, we have become the medium (and perhaps even the message). And while many theorists are frightened by the possibility of

NEW DIRECTIONS FOR TEACHING AND LEARNING, no. 94, Summer 2003 © Wiley Periodicals, Inc.

man merging with machine, others, such as Kevin Kelly (interviewed by author, September 1996), editor of *Wired* magazine, celebrate the integration of man, machine, and nature. But we are not simply message media; we are agents capable of changing our communities and ourselves. And our destiny is not simply to integrate with the grand machine of the Internet; it is, at the right moments, our destiny to detach ourselves from it and express our agency.

It is not enough to lurk and wallow in the Internet's sea of information, and it is not enough to display artistry and expertise in exploring cyberspace and constructing virtual worlds. If it were, the critics would be right: we should eschew cyberspace and "get a life!" But perhaps it isn't a matter of immersion or avoidance. Contrary to the enthusiasts who declare immersion to be inevitable, like the bee's immersion in the life of the hive, technology can be a catalyst that implements our free will. We do have a choice about whether and when to log on, or what to do when we get there. So free will and individual moral responsibility are not virtues that can be ascribed only to Luddites, any more than they are quaint notions to be left behind by the enthusiastic explorers of cyberspace. Responsible choices will lead us into some quarters of cyberspace, and they will lead us out again, enriched, instructed, and better equipped to be agents of constructive change. Clearly, though, speculation about the new technologies, virtual reality, and virtual community is a daunting task—in some ways like the lot of the ancient Milesian philosophers, who, over two thousand years ago, began thinking systematically about the nature of reality and of Plato and those who followed him in reflecting on Utopia, the idea of existence, and the perfect city.

Critics of technology do not really object to all technology; they are not interested in returning to prewheel, prefire days. The critics object, rather, to modern technology—especially to artifacts of industrial and postindustrial epochs, such as factories and computers. But those who embrace technology with an excess of enthusiasm look forward to technologies—especially computer technology, knitting us together in such a way that a novel group mind emerges. Perhaps neither extreme adequately describes our encounter with cyberspace and its technology. Therefore, it is possible that cyberspace can be colonized with Thoreauvian inwardness without shirking society by retreating to Walden Pond and without abandoning the values of the natural world. We have to find a middle ground.

What is important about these musings is that what we decide to do with our tools will in effect paint the collage of our future. We need to understand when to log on and when to log off—and why. Most people find themselves in the back seat of a car going much too fast as the media bombards them with the notion that if they don't get on the Information Superhighway in a hurry, they will be left behind in the dust. No one seems to ask why. Often, we have no idea why we should be buying that computer or a faster modem, subscribing to AOL, or buying a variety of hardware and software. And we rarely ask ourselves how doing any of this might change our lives. It is possible that if we begin to address this question, we might be able to make informed, well-grounded, and intelligent decisions about how and why we might integrate these new technologies into our lives.

Conversations

We cannot ignore the transformation taking place in our world today—the fact that the new technologies and the associated dramatic changes in the relationship between people and information are creating the cultural signature of the world. We are in the midst of a revolution that will profoundly alter how we learn, work, and communicate, and conversations emerge about philosophical considerations inherent in the use of these technologies. These conversations, however, are rarely heard in the halls of the U.S. Department of Defense, a place where people grasp at faster, more powerful, larger models of technology. Nor are they always found in the midst of such enterprises as Disney Studios, which counts on speed, higher resolution, better animation, and other gadgets to enhance its designs.

The conversation is alive in the field of education, but, too often, it is centered on technology's being a "quick fix" for the ills of our educational system, be it at the kindergarten or the college level—or at any point in between. For instance, by looking for instant gratification, we commit huge amounts of money to computer labs for schools, failing in the process of understanding why we are doing so. Neil Postman (1995) posits that we no longer have an answer for the question Why? He also suggests that there is no longer a driving narrative (or story) that guides our educational system. Yet he says that we are often turning toward technology for renewal. He cautions that "the role that new technology should play in our schools. . . . is something that needs to be discussed without the hyperactive fantasies of cheerleaders" (p. 41). In other words, he recommends that we talk and think seriously about what technology can provide us with within the framework of sound educational philosophy.

Some writers are convinced that "the Net generation" has arrived. Don Tapscott (1998) addresses the need to rethink and reenvision our educational system to meet the needs of children who have grown up surrounded by digital media. Much of this thinking revolves around what technology *does* to us. However, a new voice has turned this notion upside down. Robert Pool (1997) suggests that society might actually shape technology. He indicates that we have by necessity been narrow in our approach to understanding new technologies. Perhaps who we are as a people and as a society has always been instrumental in guiding the design of what we build.

Educators are heard discussing the need to integrate technology into the classroom in a variety of arenas. If you subscribe to listservs about education, you will find that the emphasis is on hardware, software, connectivity, and, sometimes, pedagogy. And even those constrained to discussing teaching and learning take the new technologies for granted; they do not question the presence of technology but talk about how to adapt to it. Some dialogue appears in academic journals, and it ranges from stories by faculty members about a particular project to discussions about the value of a Web-based piece of software. The conversations are also found in the midst of professional development circles. Everyone in the education business appears to be learning a new skill, getting a computer into his or her classroom, and encouraging students to go online. The emphasis here, however, is often primarily on skills development rather than on educational philosophy or integration for the purpose of enhancing learning. And, of course, the conversation goes on in whispers between teachers who are trying to meet standards, be on the cutting edge, learn what they can, and integrate new tools within their classrooms. Yet some are intimidated by the enormous task and the necessary skills, and they often lack real support as they are already overwhelmed by the business of teaching and learning with students.

Perhaps we need to look at all of this a bit differently—that is, view technology as a catalyst rather than as a solution. Technology is a catalyst, in that it affords all of us an opportunity to revisit how, what, and why we are teaching. The conversation needs to make the leap from the question What kind of software is that? to the question What kind of critical thinking skills are being developed by the use of that software? More important, we can't take for granted that just any software or technology will successfully meet our goals. Therefore, the conversations triggered by the new communication technologies can become complex avenues in the analysis of our strategies for teaching, learning, and living. Technology is also a catalyst for change because, in our struggle to master its use, we have by necessity become learners. Our students' technological skills are often more advanced, and we must allow ourselves to learn from them. This affords us the opportunity to be in touch with how it feels to be on the other end of the teaching/learning spectrum.

We certainly don't want to enter into a contract with the new technologies and then leave behind what we have come to consider sound pedagogy. To this end, we should be reminded of the seven principles of good practice as they relate to technology. Chickering and Ehrmann (1996) suggest that "any given instructional strategy can be supported by a number of contrasting technologies" and that sound educational practice is what should drive the method. Thus, they recommend frequent student-faculty contact, using a team approach with students, active learning strategies, and feedback loops between students and the faculty—raising the bar and making the expectations high, as well as creating an educational atmosphere that respects diverse talents, intelligences, and learning styles (Chickering and Ehrmann, 1996).

The chapters in this volume might help articulate how we can understand technology as a catalyst for change and how it can support our desire to revolutionize (or renew) our educational system. The contributions highlight both philosophical and practical approaches to the inclusion—or exclusion—of technology.

New Metaphors

A theme that runs through all of the chapters in this volume is that of new metaphors. Technology is guiding our experience through the metaphors we create to explain it. It might be Kevin Kelly's view of people coming together in a hive mind, or perhaps our look at the future through watching *Star Trek* and *Blade Runner*. One can also look through any magazine today and be bombarded with advertisements making predictions about lifestyles of the twenty-first century, or the new millennium, or the future, or whatever name is given to what comes next.

We are inundated with images, icons, notions, and words that have suddenly crept into our vocabularies. What are we doing about this? How can we look at the events that appear to be shaping our future, and how can we have some say about how and when they might occur? After all, it is our students who are the Net generation, the visual learners by and large, the media groupies, the ones whose view of the future is guided more by those television commercials and science fiction films than by our attempt to provide them with direction within an educational environment.

In Chapter Two, Megumi Taniguchi takes into consideration the power of metaphors. She presents a case for language as metaphor—in particular, our language about technology actually guiding the way we view it. She analyzes the metaphors we use (such as scanning the Web, cruising the Information Superhighway, or surfing the Internet), and she suggests that these contribute to our conceptualization of technology, especially in educational venues. Convinced that the power of metaphors transforms our understanding of concepts, Taniguchi suggests that the metaphors have both students and teachers believing that the Internet is far more information-inclusive than it truly is. Thus, our expectations of the technology are somewhat influenced by the language we use to describe it. In order to correct this, Taniguchi creatively proposes a set of new metaphors that might better represent the reality of how we navigate or use technology in our lives.

In contrast to Taniguchi, Randy Hensley (Chapter Three) is clear that new metaphors must be discovered and embraced to inform us about the new role of libraries in our educational environments. He states that the traditional library as place is obsolete. Although, obviously, this has not yet occurred, many people now use the Internet as a reference tool. Just a generation ago, they would have gone to the library for information, but information is now at their fingertips. Hensley suggests that the library has always been seen as a place, but now a new technology-driven environment can be viewed as the same kind of "place." His theory, however, is much more than just a transfer of place from building to virtual space. Hensley suggests that we accept a more profound metaphor to explain how we choose to navigate through information.

Totally upending traditional notions of teaching and learning, David Wolsk, in Chapter Ten, offers a new metaphor—one that does not depend on technology at all—or on what we consider the "usual" trajectory of learning. He finds that there is a world outside the classroom, which should be integrated into the pedagogy of teaching and learning. He suggests that we lose much if we start with textbooks, lectures, and traditional schooling. Wolsk would like to see education begin with real-world experiences—the driving narrative being life itself. Technology could help mediate this, or it could further alienate students from life.

Tools

Another theme to consider is that of *tools*. Is technology a tool or a medium? Does it alter the way we think? Are we in control of our tools? Can we be? Have we become sidetracked by this new technology and now find ourselves teaching Computer? Did we ever teach Pencil? Stapler? Crayons? No. We taught how to write, how to fasten paper together, how to color pretty pictures. We need to understand the difference between teaching the application(s) of a tool and teaching the tool. This may seem obvious. However, with the rampant purchase of computer equipment, much of the focus has been on teaching the tool, to either the faculty or to students. This sometimes allows the tools to drive the activities.

Kevin Kelly warned against jumping in too soon and about spending too much money on new tools before being clear about what they can do for us. He suggested that technology is more powerful than we think; it is more extensive and more humanizing. And, contrary to George Orwell's depiction of our future world, technology is going to move from the monolithic, centralized, and brutish image to one that is softer and more human (interview with author, September 1996). Certainly, to date, the new technologies, unlike a hammer, are not as transparent as we would wish them to be. We walk into a room and expect there to be a light switch on the wall and think nothing of reaching and turning it on. Computer technology is still something we think about rather than use as a matter of course. But this is changing, and, as it does, it will change the landscape of higher education.

Barry Maid, in Chapter Four, discusses what technology might or might not contribute to teaching and learning in higher education. He grapples with how the academy functions (which is slowly), and he wonders how it will be possible for decisions to be made in a timely fashion. He also addresses funding issues, philosophical crossroads between the academy and the rest of the world, and the fact that in the final analysis, decisions should be driven by the desire to teach well.

In Chapter Five, Wesley Cooper traces the manner in which he came to embrace the new technologies in his educational endeavors. His spirited and candid description of his discovery and how this has actually changed how much time he spends on teaching shows how a revolution might be taking place—one faculty member at a time.

Communication and Community

Two other themes are significant to understanding the effects of technology in our society: communication and community. How have the new technologies changed our lives? Is that cell phone or pager in your pocket something that has made life better? Are we empowering those who most often don't have access to power in our society? Or are we further alienating them? Does the ability to access global communications create people who are more open and free with their ideas? Is an e-mail to a colleague in Russia much better than a snail mail letter to a colleague in Russia? New tools offer many options with which to communicate more efficiently, develop projects that are global, and bring people together. But all of this only works if the person designing the activity is willing to define the outcomes.

The concept of *community* has been addressed by a variety of sociologists, anthropologists, philosophers, and theorists. Some say that technology is destroying community; others contend that it extends and strengthens it. What is the definition of community? What exactly are the elements that one finds in a community? What brings people together? Is it more than a shared place? Shared values? Language? Ray Oldenburg (1989) suggests that we have always had three places we would define as our community: home, work, and a third place. This third place used to be the malt shop, a corner on Main Street, the pub, or some other public gathering place; people would migrate to these places for social discourse. One way to look at cyberspace is as another place to gather. Taken in that light, is it possible that community is now extended beyond our physical borders? We need to talk about why communities come together in the first place. Do they have to be temporal? Is it a bad sign if a community disbands? What is different about communities in cyberspace? Are we now being asked to be members of a wide range of communities? Do we introduce our students to the opportunities inherent in this variety? And what are virtual communities anyway? How do they form? Why do they form? Answers to these questions will guide us as we define for ourselves emerging communities, made possible by new technologies.

Howard Rheingold, widely known as the editor of *The Millennium Whole Earth Catalog* (1995) and author of *Virtual Reality: The Revolutionary Technology of Computer-Generated Artificial Worlds* (1992) and *The Virtual Community: Homesteading on the Electronic Frontier* (1994, 2000), defined community as a place where people share an interest and have conversations and relationships that take place over time. He suggested that what connects us to America, for instance, is an idea, and in a virtual community, what connects people is also an idea—a shared interest or goal (interviewed by author, June 1996). However, many people argue that modern life might begin to become modem life (or cable life)—lonely and alienating. Computer technology allows people to stay at home, alone, in front of a blue flickering screen (not unlike the television) and thus find themselves in ultimate seclusion and estrangement. It is also possible, though, to imagine that this blue screen, rather than alienating people, actually brings people together, creating new spaces, new villages.

In Chapter Six, Stephen Romanoff examines how the new technologies have offered communication possibilities to build a virtual learning community. Romanoff shares the details of a cross-continent project that brought together students who would never have met otherwise. His article has implications for a more global approach to teaching and learning. He finds that the principles of good teaching and learning can be enhanced by the use of technology, if done appropriately.

Another interesting manner in which online education builds community is described in the case study by Margit Misangyi Watts on service learning. In Chapter Seven, Watts illustrates how taking a course online and mentoring students who are in turn working within the community on service learning projects serves to build connections. The places her students gather are in cyberspace as well as in physical spaces. In this way the online environment augments more traditional teaching methods.

Learning

Concerning *learning,* it is probably most useful to ask the question What are we learning about learning when using technology? Though not actually talking about technology, Ellen Langer (1997) considers learning myths and suggests that we must rethink what it is to learn. Langer suggests a "mindful approach" to learning, advising us to question *why* we do what we do, and, more specifically, what our approach means for learning (p. 2).

Seymour Papert (1993), however, sees new opportunities afforded by computer technology. He hopes that we can focus on learning rather than on teaching. He suggests that "pedagogy, the art of teaching, under its various names, has been adopted by the academic world as a respectable and important field. The art of learning is an academic orphan" (p. 82). He asks some important questions, such as, "Does school utilize the way human beings most naturally learn in a nonschool setting?" (p. 5). Does technology put the learner in the driver's seat?

Michael Bertsch (Chapter Eight) is quite excited about the new possibilities that technology offers the art of learning. His interest is in the idea of text immersion as possibly the best way to learn writing. Bertsch finds online environments to be excellent venues for text immersion, allowing for a great deal of practice in a judgment-free and academically safe educational space. And Wesley Cooper presents, in Chapter Nine, a new twist on the study of philosophy. He acknowledges that this is a new field for philosophers and then presents a case study of how he uses virtual environments to teach his course.

Narratives

Neil Postman (1995) has concluded that today we no longer have a driving narrative to inform our educational practice. He finds that we do not really know how to answer the question Why? As educators, we have spent the last twenty years discussing the how and what of teaching. What is the best way to teach history? What pieces of literature do we include in our English classes? And so on. We enter into serious dialogue about why we are doing any of this whenever we decide to change the general education requirements at a college or university. But we don't ever bring the conversation of delivery methods into the mix. If we begin to do so, we will be designing effective educational models. Then and only then can we begin to see how the new technologies can be a catalyst for improvement. For example, the use of technology might actually help with a constructivist approach to teaching and learning—one in which students take ownership of their learning.

In the concluding chapter of this volume, Watts addresses the need for higher education to integrate two strong narratives, which are competing for attention. Colleges are restructuring their general education requirements, retraining faculty in the art of active teaching and learning models, and trying to personalize the academic experience for students. At the same time, they are heading quickly toward the distance learning bandwagon. The reader is asked to keep in mind the dichotomy between these two initiatives on campuses nationwide:—the one that includes learning communities and addresses the personalization and integration of the curriculum and that of online models that use the new technologies but are seemingly in direct opposition to the first imperative. She suggests that on the one hand, we are attempting to close the gap between teacher and student, and on the other hand, we are developing online models that are not only called distance education but are considered distant in every way. Computer technologies can be used as supportive learning environments as long as solid pedagogy and educational philosophy guide their development.

Conclusion

Stephen Johnson (1997) suggests that there is "a funny thing about the fusion of technology and culture. . . . and that it has been a part of human experience since the first cave painter, but we've had a hard time seeing it until now" (p. 2). Do we see it now? Can we have a dialogue to help us understand the fusion of our tools and who we are?

If we don't, we are left spending our time on keyboarding skills, Web design, the use of e-mail, word processing, software for art and music, the creation of online courses, the digitizing of our books and ideas, and purchase of the latest and newest tool that has been made—which helps the economy. This is all valuable, but it should not be done blindly; the whole community should engage in the conversations. Rather than being caught in a web of increasing speed, wires, bells, and whistles, let's begin by asking why as often as possible. And when the answer is sufficiently clear, we can then spend time on the implementation and the content. By taking control of our tools, we have a better chance of taking control of our future.

References

Chickering, A. W., and Ehrmann, S. C. "Implementing the Seven Principles: Technology as Lever." *AAHE Bulletin,* Oct. 1996.

Johnson, S. *Interface Culture: How New Technology Transforms the Way We Create and Communicate.* San Francisco: HarperEdge, 1997.

Langer, E. J. *The Power of Mindful Learning.* Reading, Mass.: Addison-Wesley, 1997.

Oldenburg, R. *The Great Good Place.* New York: Marlowe, 1989.

Papert, S. *The Children's Machine: Rethinking School in the Age of the Computer.* New York: Basic Books, 1993.

Pool, R. *Beyond Engineering: How Society Shapes Technology.* New York: Oxford University Press, 1997.

Postman, N. *The End of Education.* New York: Knopf, 1995.

Tapscott, D. *Growing Up Digital: The Rise of the Net Generation.* New York: McGraw-Hill, 1998.

MARGIT MISANGYI WATTS is director of Rainbow Advantage/Freshman Seminars at the University of Hawaii at Manoa. She is active in the national movement for information literacy, is involved in campus initiatives in distance learning, and recently wrote a text for first-year students, College: We Make the Road by Walking.

2

Computer metaphors are taken for granted and thus powerfully guide the way in which teachers work with students. Redefinition of our guiding metaphor is vital in taking the distance out of education.

Internet Metaphors Matter

Megumi I. Taniguchi

Theorists who have commented on computer technology have repeatedly commented on how language (and language about technology) is, in many ways, metaphorical. Whether we are aware of it or not, our metaphors about technology affect the way(s) in which we view it. Lakoff and Johnson (1980) point out that although metaphor seems to be an artificial construct (reminiscent only of poetry classes and comparisons with similes), it is a vital way of reenvisioning the world and is thus quite central to our understanding. Metaphor is, after all, at its most basic, a description of one thing by another. Computer metaphors have become so prevalent in the media (commercials, print ads, talk shows) that they have been burned into our collective subconscious. As a result, metaphors about the Internet—such as scanning the Web, unifying the Global Village, cruising on the Information Superhighway, and surfing the Net—have become standard expressions overnight. We no longer give computer metaphors a second thought, much less question them because they simply are a part of reality. Thus, they play a much larger part in our conceptualizations of technology than we realize. Nowhere is this more apparent than in educational contexts.

Basic Metaphors

The power of metaphor originates in its ability to transform our understanding of concepts, ideas, and forms. Names of objects may not seem important, but they have an undeniable impact on the way the objects are perceived. Metaphors dealing with the Internet have hit the mainstream and are perhaps some of the most important and heavily used technological metaphors today. There are four basic metaphors for the Internet: we say that we are looking information up on the Web, making the most of the

Global Village, traveling on an Information Superhighway, or surfing the Net. These metaphors all call to mind very different images and present vastly divergent ways of viewing computer technology. These metaphors are so prevalent and recognizable, and so deeply ingrained in our minds, that it is difficult not to slip into using one of them. Thus, even these metaphors—don't get left behind on the Information Superhighway, surfing the Net, and catch the right waves—have quickly become clichés.

The first metaphor, the Web, seems the most innocuous, and descriptive of the group. It should be pointed out that the Web and the Internet are often used interchangeably but are quite distinct, since the Web refers to a "unifying force, a system that would seamlessly bind all file-protocols into a single point of access" (Zhou, 2000, p. 50), whereas the Internet refers to the separate network systems. At first glance, a web and a net are a lot alike; they both catch things—in computer terms, information. The metaphor seems to appealingly describe the way in which all the Web sites—indeed, all parts of the Internet—connect.

The Web is often touted as an important source of (or trap for) information, which would seem to imply that it was set up for educational purposes, to be a comprehensive information-gathering device. It is true that the delivery of information has been its main goal, but the original intent was to create a communications system for the military, able to deliver or reroute information from an array of sources. The main problem with teaching students the web metaphor is that it obscures this limitation. In addition, it misrepresents their role with the Internet, since they tend to be passive recipients rather than active researchers, and it oversimplifies the process of gathering information.

The second metaphor, the Global Village, credited to McLuhan and Powers (1989), is very similar to Rheingold's virtual community metaphor (1994): technology is portrayed as a unifying and encompassing force that allows people around the world access to differing points of view. This metaphor envisions a positive, democratic world system that operates on mutual respect, communication, and understanding. The Global Village ideal was quickly adapted and used as an appealing marketing tool to advertise new technologies. This metaphor seems to indicate that all the information in the world is just a few mouse clicks away. Teachers may not overtly use this term when they teach, but their own thinking may be guided by this harmonious image of computer use.

Teachers can thus overlook the inherent complexities of Internet usage. Crystal (2001) has done a comprehensive look at the linguistic implications of the Internet. He points out that "if we cannot discern any unifying dialect or language, or a trend towards such unity, we need to ask ourselves if this 'global village' is anything more than a media fiction" (p. 6). Resnick (1997) notes that the image of a "huge but close-knit community that shares common values and experiences" is "misleading" because "many cultures coexist on the Internet and at times clash" (p. 62). He goes on to suggest that the concept of a city, "with its suggestion of unlimited opportunities and myriad dangers" (p. 62), is closer to the image we seek. It is true that while Internet interactions can be glowing, hand-holding ventures, they can also be negative exchanges made up of arguments, squabbling, soapbox declarations, and even flaming. On more than one occasion, I have spoken to students who were asked to observe a listserv on a given topic and then write up their reactions. The level of conflict and contention that they encountered took these students aback. One student commented, "But I thought they were supposed to be professional. I certainly didn't expect that, and I got so sick of it I couldn't listen to it anymore!"

The frequency with which the third ubiquitous metaphor, the Information Superhighway, is used seems to indicate that it dominates our view. One explanation for this that Slouka (1995) and others advance is that it presents one version of the American Dream. Although it may be true that the Information Superhighway offers speed, efficiency, and "on-ramps" for education, it is not without its share of complications and potential problems. Information offered on the Internet is of uneven quality and thus needs to be researched more thoroughly. Students must learn new skills and strategies for research, and, more important, for thinking. The Internet is able to offer recent, updated information, but it can overwhelm students with information, which students do not always have the determination to sift through or analyze. The fourth, more colloquial, metaphor, surfing the Net, seems at first glance to be a stilted and contrived combination of words. But it also presents another version of the American Dream in its youthful, highly individualistic and physical pursuit of adventure. Surfers' decisions, timing, skill, experience, and willingness to face risks determine the outcome of each set. Students are a good target audience for this metaphor.

The smiling, motivated students shown in computer ads, who zip from one Web site to the next, seem to imply that there are no boundaries to limit where you can go. To be fair, it must be pointed out that this positive image is not completely illusory. The Web has afforded students many opportunities to venture beyond the classroom in the form of posting essays, drawings, and photos, communicating with others, and creating Web pages.

Yet the reality is sometimes far from the dream. One article states, "Know why it's called 'surfing the net'? Because it's like riding a rogue wave—you never know where the search engine is going to take you" ("How to Search Smarter," 1995, p. 155). The verb *surfing* also troubles some, who feel that the metaphor interferes with educational uses of the Internet. Day (1996), for example, proposes that teachers substitute the term *skimming* for surfing. He points out that "SURFING isn't quite the right analogy for the behavior we need to encourage in students. It reeks too much of the outcast and maverick, or of someone who might just ride right over a lot of good information without seeing it" (p. 4). The problem is that students are affected by industry slogans such as "Where Do You Want to Go

Today?" and they often read the hidden subtext, which claims that you can go anywhere using a computer.

I once had an experience in which I stumbled across a group of glassy-eyed students who had spent several hours trying to find on the computer information on the life span of various animals. When I asked them whether they had checked the encyclopedia, they seemed to dismiss it as a silly question. Clearly, though, it would have been much faster to flip open an encyclopedia. Ironically, they were able to find the life span of a nene goose (the indigenous state bird of Hawaii) on the computer but not that of some of the more common animals. They were actually stuck, trying to figure out what a certain abbreviation meant. The Web site had the abbreviation asterisked but never provided a definition, and the students searched linking pages in vain. This anecdote suggests the expectations that students develop. They were shocked not to find a Web page about their specific topic and were sure it must be *somewhere* out there. This may seem to be an isolated experience, but it has been my experience with students. I have seen students even question whether something really exists if they can't find it on the Internet, or they stop to question the correct spelling of a word if they can't find any information about it on the Internet.

Limitations of These Metaphors

Academics are currently struggling with the ways in which they present the Web to their students. In an educational sense, the main problem is that all the current metaphors seem to engender passive feelings of acceptance by both educators and students. Internet and Web metaphors suggest that it is possible to capture everything—or almost everything. The Information Superhighway and surfing metaphors suggest that all you need is the right equipment to go flying along. Yet it is clear that these images don't tell the whole story. Keeping track of what is on the Internet, much less cataloguing all of it, is an impossible feat at best. Although search engines are constantly being upgraded and improved, there are still concerns about their use. Search engines can currently index basic information contained on Web sites, but they still lack the sophistication to match human indexing capabilities (Lynch, 1997). As students become experts in navigating on the Web, they realize that the Internet is not the end-all and be-all source of information, and they will be able to ascertain that the Internet is only one of myriad sources.

The hype surrounding computers is powerful and the metaphors created in relation to them fuel the fervor for computers. Some educators (many unwittingly) are complicitous in making every attempt to use computers, assuming that any use of them by the students must be positive. Sadly, instructors who use word processing or e-mail to freewrite—when writing by hand would be less time-consuming and would ultimately serve the same purpose—are missing the point. Technology can provide students with excellent opportunities, but technology for technology's sake should be questioned. Some educators proudly announce that they have all their students do Web sites. When they are asked the purpose of the Web sites, these educators are initially at a loss for words but then quickly declare, "We do Web sites!" Many teachers will readily maintain the idea that the educational purpose or intent of any lesson should always be established and made clear to the students. Yet this sentiment can be lost in the face of technology. The stakes are high, and there is prestige and recognition associated with technology, so educators eagerly purchase expensive computer equipment and software for their students. Sometimes, educators do not know enough about the technology to anticipate what types of software will serve their students' needs best. The alarming part is that students subconsciously seem to make the connection that the Information Superhighway supercedes books, journals, and other more traditional sources of information. They feel that if computers open up a highway, books can only offer bumpy roads, slow indexes, and outdated information. To put it in metaphoric terms, many of us do not bother to question highways, we just use them. After all, doesn't it make sense to use the fastest mode of transportation? The answer is, not always. If an accident occurs that closes all lanes of traffic, it may be more beneficial to travel on backroads.

If educators stop to think about it, many who were raised with the various types of media will realize that computers may not be the best source of information. True, the Internet can be an excellent source of breaking information. Students may be able to find the most current information on new topics, such as road rage or the latest rock band, before books, journals, and television are able to report on them. But the Internet is not always the best source for older information that may be duplicated elsewhere or may prove confusing and might actually confound searches for specific information. Indeed, the abundance of information that is sometimes available can overwhelm students, and there is no guarantee that the first ten pages that are listed will yield the information they need. I've also had students tell me that they figured out that using the first ten sites would yield the best information, so they stopped after that without skimming any others to see what types of information they might offer.

Like any other source, the Internet has its limitations. The world of computers is currently more confusing than many are willing to acknowledge. The Information Superhighway is a hodgepodge of different types of information. On the one hand, it does have glitzy sites with many links and highly informative pages, and if students have access to sound, video capabilities, and special frame features, the possibilities do seem endless. On the other hand, the Information Superhighway has more dead ends, roadblocks, and construction projects than most people realize. Pages are not always maintained or updated, there is outdated information, and Web pages move or disappear. Sources may be unreliable or questionable.

The Information Superhighway may also present unresearched ideas and personal opinion as fact. Up until college, many students seem to assume that if something is printed, it is factual; if it's written down, it must be true. But, as educators, we cannot fault them for that. Even adults fail to stop to question urban myth-type e-mails, thus ensuring the easy circulation of fake stories. Students need to be explicitly trained in the correct use of the Internet. In college, one skill that students must learn is that all information must be verified. Because the Information Superhighway presents both personal opinion and fact, students are unable to differentiate between commentaries and factual reports. Unlike newspapers, which provide categories such as letters to the editor, editorials, and news briefs, the lines on the Internet blur. Although many celebrate the supposed equal access the Web provides as a positive attribute, the Web allows anyone (with the desire to create a page, Internet knowhow, and a service provider to upload information to the Internet) to say anything he or she wants to say. On many pages, the author is not readily identified, so it is difficult and sometimes impossible to verify the credibility of a given source.

Ultimately, it is just too simplistic to say that this new source of information is a better medium. Yes, it definitely has the potential to be a wonderful learning tool, but educators must realize that the effective use of computers is made only when they stop to assess why they are using computers in any given case. Educators must teach their students new skills to facilitate learning. How you search and what you search for are just as important and ultimately influence where you want to go. Many Web search engines provide ways to refine searches, but it is unlikely that students who are unsure of how to navigate the Internet in the first place will figure out how to do so on their own. Educators' use of technology and technological metaphors constantly need to be assessed and evaluated.

New Metaphors

By renaming, we reenvision and thus take creative control of our own perceptions. I offer three possible metaphors for the Internet here:

1. The Trail. If we remain predisposed to use a Super Information Highway exploration theme, a trail would not be such a bad metaphor. Logic tells us that only well-experienced, licensed drivers are allowed access to highways. The Internet does not connote any similar sense of responsibility. In contrast, trails are man-made creations, and by definition, they offer one possible way (of many) in an implied forest of possibilities. Trails can be well established or freshly created, which parallels the huge range from well-maintained sites to here today, gone tomorrow sites. The metaphor slows the student down long enough for her to realize the intentions of her actions and the possibilities that actually exist. The road is not paved; it is created a step at a time.

This metaphor should appeal to fairy tale enthusiasts who have interpreted fairy tales as cautionary stories whose enduring appeal lies in their ability to teach and instruct. Hansel and Gretel left a trail of bread crumbs, could not find their way back, and were almost eaten by a witch. Perhaps this fairy tale is more accurate because it reinforces the responsibility of the explorer and possible dangers in the forest. Students need not avoid the Internet altogether, but they should be aware of computer scams, privacy and content issues, computer crashes, flamers, and the like.

2. Links. We may be able to substitute a term, which is already in usage, such as Link (capitalized L), for the entire network, and links (uncapitalized l) for individual Web sites. Although this term may seem no different than the Web metaphor, it defines in a less restrictive way because it offers multiple interpretations (metal link, S link, necklace link, cuff link, communication link), and in some ways, it forces the user to think about possible meanings. Grammatically, the term link can be a noun or a verb, so it can be an object or an action. Whereas a spider most often constructs a web, links are man-made. This small distinction is critical because it elucidates the fact that the Internet is a creation of human intentionality—and that, in turn, conveys a sense of responsibility. Students forge meaning to transform links into chains. Imagination propels their creations.

Links hint at connections but do not imply a complete whole. There is no beginning or end. But a web is, by definition, a defined totality. Completed, it implies some type of perfection. Each Web site, or point of union, is seen as a logical, necessary equal point in one unified whole, one parallel pattern. This does not reflect reality. The structure of the Internet, if there is such a thing, is constantly changing, altering when Web sites are removed, changed, or given new URLs. Thus, unlike a web, the Internet is hardly affected if one site disappears. In fact, that one site may not be missed by anyone. As stated previously, in contrast with webs, links do not suggest a complete entity. Instead, they perpetually offer the possibility of infinite, multiple-level connections that parallel the dynamic, expansive, random nature of the Internet. A link metaphor allows for the possibility of missing—or weak—links, which is important, as Web sites are often lost or problematic.

3. Thread/Fiber/Strand. Many individuals already use another possible metaphor. A line of inquiry formulated by an Internet discussion group is known as a thread. Use of this term—and others, such as fiber, strand, sewing with a thread, threading, determining the fiber, and following the strand—are admittedly awkward. However, it may actually help to capture some of the other attributes of the Internet. Comparing one line of discussion or one line of inquiry to a thread will help students to better visualize the scale of the Internet (made up of billions of threads, some stronger and some weaker). A thread is itself made up of other smaller threads and is therefore tenuous.

Although the thread metaphor can also lead students to believe that there is a purpose to the Internet, the thread metaphor emphasizes their agency and responsibility in creating anything. The Web metaphor already predetermines that the Web exists and that students simply have to use it. The thread metaphor, by contrast, doesn't emphasize any finished conception of the Internet. The Internet is changing so quickly (sites altering, moving, or disappearing) that any finished image of it as a highway, net, or web cannot fully capture its ever-evolving nature. This metaphor is also more in line with other educational metaphors that emphasize construction and the student's role in building an argument, supporting a view, or gathering evidence.

Conclusion

As the Internet is used more and more in classrooms, it is important that not only teachers but also students be given an opportunity to stop and think about these issues. Quick scans of the Internet reveal that some classes already do this: teachers have students examine the current Internet metaphors and develop new ones. Inventing new metaphors is a vital activity because it affords us the freedom to reinvent our ideas about technology and the ways we think about it.

I'll never forget my own experience of sitting in a computer conference many years ago and having the speaker refer to the URL as an "Earl" (rather than calling it a U-R-L). All at once, this simple reference personified the Web address term and made it less mechanical and much more accessible.

Internet metaphors do matter. If enough individuals in our society stop to question existing metaphors, conversation and discussion will be generated in meaningful ways. People no longer question that the Internet is the future, so we as a society must stop to assess our current limiting metaphors and suggest new ones to open up our own thinking about technology. For example, many have noticed that using such a term as user brings with it the connotation of drug use. Shannon proposed replacing the term with "participant. . . . to emphasize the interactive nature of the Net" (cited in Horvitz, 1997).

Renaming the Internet every month would indeed prove impractical, but reinventing its metaphors—and our limiting ideas about it—is essential. The implications of Internet metaphors already affect students and our role in education in more ways than we realize. If we can take the distance out of education by controlling metaphors, we can redefine our role as active participants and, in the process, make computer technology more accessible for students and educators alike.

References

Crystal, D. *Language and the Internet.* Cambridge: Cambridge University Press, 2001.
Day, M. "Fear and Loathing in Paradise: Making Use of Dissensus, Disorientation, and Discouragement on the Moo." Excerpted from a talk presented at conference: "The Virtual Classroom: Writing Across the Internet," Berkeley, Calif., Mar. 16, 1996.

Horvitz, L. A. "Amateur Linguistics Say Language, not Electrons, Defines Cyberspace." *Insight on the News*, Sept. 8, 1997, p. 42.

"How to Search Smarter." *Fast Company*, 1995, 5, 155.

Lakoff, G., and Johnson, M. *Metaphors We Live By*. Chicago: University of Chicago Press, 1980.

Lynch, C. "Searching the Internet." *Scientific American*, Mar. 1997, 276(3), 52.

McLuhan, M., and Powers, B. R. *The Global Village: Transformations in World Life and Media in the 21st Century*. New York: Oxford University Press, 1989.

Resnick, P. "Filtering Information on the Internet." *Scientific American*, Mar. 1997, 276(3), 62.

Rheingold, H. *The Virtual Community: Homesteading on the Electronic Frontier*. New York: HarperPerennial, 1994.

Slouka, M. *War of the Worlds: Cyberspace and the High-Tech Assault on Reality*. New York: Basic Books, 1995.

Zhou, J. "The Internet, the World Wide Web, Library Web Browsers, and Library Web Servers." *Information Technology and Libraries*, Mar. 2000, p. 50.

MEGUMI I. TANIGUCHI is an academic adviser for the Colleges of Arts and Sciences Student Academic Services at the University of Hawaii at Manoa. She co-coordinates the First-Year Center, a resource center for incoming freshmen and transfer students. She previously taught English composition at the college level.

3

When technology is used as an environment for learning rather than as an instrument of learning, it begins to look feel, smell, and act like a pretechnology library.

Technology as Environment: From Collections to Connections

Randy Burke Hensley

Libraries have existed in human culture for thousands of years. As institutions with roles and functions, they have altered to meet new demands from the cultures of which they have been a part. They have occasionally suffered the slings and arrows of fortune, outrageous and otherwise. Their history has often mirrored developments in the cultures they have striven to represent, and they have been a part of most cultural shifts in one form or another. The transformation of the meaning of information, knowledge, education, and community in our late twentieth century/early twenty-first century culture affects libraries. This transformation affects how we define the purpose of libraries, how we expect them to function, and what the meaning of *library* for the culture might be in the future.

The library crisis faced by libraries obsesses the people whom the culture places in charge of the libraries: the librarians. To verify this, examine any issue of *American Libraries*, published by the American Library Association. The library crisis is a crisis of meaning and purpose, and it is the result of the emergence of cyberculture. Cultural transformation causes changes in institutions that survive the transformation and causes the elimination of institutions that do not change. Libraries ought to survive, but to do so, major changes are required.

In order to identify what libraries should be, we start with what they are broadly understood to be at the present time. First, libraries are collections of tangible artifacts, and, for the most part, these artifacts are books. The twentieth century produced additional artifacts that libraries collect, but most library collections emphasize printed text. The Latin derivation of the word *library* is "of books."

NEW DIRECTIONS FOR TEACHING AND LEARNING, no. 94, Summer 2003 © Wiley Periodicals, Inc. 23

Second, until the advent of the free public library in the United States, the history of libraries meant selective access to the collection that a library comprised. The word *patron* is still used to refer to the user of a library in the United States. Patron implies a supporter and a regular client. There is regular discussion among librarians about the accuracy of this term to describe individuals who use their libraries. Many librarians do not think patron accurately describes a library user who makes use of an institution that allows unfettered access to its collection.

Third, libraries select the collection, not selecting everything that is published. Some libraries have very sharp and distinct selection rules, and a library controls the collection through a variety of mechanisms, such as circulation limits, availability limits, and methods of making known to the library user what is available. Both the card catalogue and its technological offspring, the online catalogue, have protocols for what an individual can know about what the library collects.

Fourth, libraries are physical places. The library is tangible. What a library does and how it does it is limited to a geographical location.

Pretechnology Library

The pretechnology library enabled exploration. Many a senior faculty member will tell you about the glory days of browsing the shelves or the thrill of perusing archival materials to discover the unknown piece of correspondence. The technology that has increasingly taken over our culture's notions of where knowledge is kept and found can also be approached with that sense of impending discovery, where the process is the answer. The extent to which information literacy is about rekindling that appreciation for process and engaging the formation of personal meaning is the source of its relevance to the educational process. And an emphasis on process is necessarily also an emphasis on engagement.

The pretechnology library was about discovery. There were catalogues and indexes, but their primary function was to identify a place to begin. Getting to the collection so that browsing could occur—through shelves, stacks of journals, or file cabinets—was the primary function. Catalogues, indexes, and abstracts created structures that supported the browsing process. Broad subject headings, references, and disciplinary topic organization encouraged users to look around and find personal meaning through examination of the options. Classification systems were used to find general areas from which the individual examination of books could occur.

Librarians served as intermediaries not so much for their subject knowledge as for their collection knowledge, what the library had available and where it was located. Librarians used their experience with knowledge browsers to create additional ways to organize libraries in order to facilitate this mode of finding. Special collections of resources organized by category proliferated. Archival and regional resources are but two examples.

Today's Library

The last twenty years have seen immense changes in library operations regarding provisioning the culture with information. The introduction of Web-based platforms for information dissemination has resulted in online catalogues, full-text article databases, and the use of Internet opportunities to access and disseminate all kinds of information—in print, visual, and audio. Libraries have forged new relationships with information creators in order to establish a segue between the traditional business of providing books published by others and the new business of providing Internet resources created by others.

Technology alters the notion of ownership. For some, the library is less a repository of uniquely possessed resources and more a gateway to a constantly increasing ocean of resources "out there." Ironically, the intersection of technology and the information explosion creates a perspective on library use that diminishes the expectation that time, effort, and process produces the best result. Instead, one assumes that the exact answer is there and that it can be found quickly.

CyberLibrary

The contrast between these traditional elements of the library and comparable elements of cyberculture reveals the transformation the library faces. First, cyberculture views information not as artifact but as a digital flow— the movement of bytes moving and coagulating periodically in time and space.

Second, cyberculture consists of participants, logging on and off, through various mechanisms of their own choosing in an individualized and collaborative fashion.

Third, individuals are perceived in cyberculture as the primary agents for authenticating and controlling the digital flow. The individual desires maximum authority over the creation and use of this flow, unfettered by filters or regulation. And finally, cyberculture is unlimited by physical space as we traditionally understand it.

With this contrast between the traditional library and the cyberlibrary in mind, the current and future definitions of information, knowledge, education, and community further illuminate the dilemma of the library. Prior to the information explosion of the twentieth century, information came in fairly distinct forms, was produced by identifiable agents, and, at intervals, appeared to be conducive to the possibility that some measure of comprehensiveness could be achieved.

Knowledge—if understood to be an acquaintance with facts, truths, and principles, or if understood as erudition acquired through study and research—had an element of hierarchy or authority. The implication in the traditional notions of knowledge was that it was at least somewhat fixed and could be arrived at through a process of the acquisition of an ultimately finite entity. Education was the process of acquiring knowledge. Historically, this process was prescribed, and access to it was limited in a number of ways. Community was most commonly understood to be a social grouping noted for attributes that provided coherence and stability over time.

Community-Defined Similarities and Boundaries

The library was guided by principles and activities that allowed it to collect information in a manner to ensure that a reasonable percentage of a culture's information artifacts would be available to its community, which was also defined by a fairly specific number of criteria. Knowledge as it has been understood could be routinely supported through the authentication and control functions of the library. Education could also be supported by libraries by means of these generalized efforts or through the specific designation of a library as a school or academic library, distinctly positioned to serve a component of the educational institution.

Libraries in the culture described were able to expand their collections in keeping with the information artifacts being produced and increase access to those collections through changes that included free public libraries, more direct access to collections, and the development of a credentialing process, whereby increased numbers of professional employees were available to create the library and provide assistance to library users not considered "elitist."

Technology at first offered solutions to managing the trends associated with an accelerating of the production of information and an expanding definition of community. Online catalogues and databases were developed to accelerate the process of making collections available, increasing the capacity of these collection control mechanisms, and expanding the community of people who could use the library. Technology facilitated cooperation among libraries as well, allowing access to collections not owned by a particular library.

However, as the information explosion continued, libraries were not able to maintain their traditional role of control through the creation of the means of that control—the catalogues and databases. Increasingly, the databases and catalogues were purchased from publishers, or the library paid for access to the record of available resources. As these resources became complete texts rather than listings of publications, the library grew more dependent on resources other than its own to be what it had understood itself to be.

Carola Stoffle, Robert Renaud, and Jerilyn Veldof (1996) articulate how these changes were linked to a growing public concern regarding the accountability of tax-supported institutions. They point to the additional issue of the accelerating costs of the libraries' resources, as well as shifts in the expectations of the library's users regarding access to collections and service.

The most disturbing element in the library crisis arose as a result of these factors, in combination with the emergence of cyberculture. As libraries began to falter in their traditional function, individuals raised the question of libraries' viability in any form. Even in the face of federal government funding for connecting libraries to the Internet, a debate was accelerated as to the question of the need for libraries in a culture where all information is digital and accessible through the World Wide Web. William Miller (1997) refutes the idea that all information is available digitally now or in the foreseeable future. He then articulates the costs of digitalizing information sources, both for current information artifacts and for the retrospective conversion of information sources not currently in that form.

The inability of the library to successfully perform its traditional function is driven by the same factors that have contributed to the development of cyberculture. These factors involve changes in the culture's understanding of information, knowledge, education, and community.

Information is an ever-increasing and accelerating phenomenon consisting of a differentiating array of forms, some traditional artifacts, and some more ephemeral but no less valuable, given the new definition of information: data flow. Education becomes a process far more collaborative than hierarchical, occurring sometimes in institutions but without regard to a particular age period in one's life. Though it is overused, the phrase *lifelong learning* defines what education is becoming: a process that occurs throughout one's life, designed to enable individuals to thrive in a culture of constant and accelerating change. Knowledge becomes more applied. Knowledge becomes facts, and truths and principles are deemed the most relevant when they can be consistently applied to long-term anticipated needs or applied to existing needs. Community becomes a social group consisting of those who affiliate for specific purposes or functions, and it is stable for the duration of that purpose. Community is not exclusively defined by geography.

Learning and Libraries

What has happened to process in libraries has happened to process in education. Learning is about distillation and synthesis. Distance learning modalities exemplify this approach. However, active learning approaches to pedagogy and content offer an intriguing antidote to the diminishment of process in both learning and libraries.

One way to think of education from an active learning perspective is to think of it as a design process involving student experience, practice, and application. Regardless of content, active learning provides opportunities for students to connect their experiences in the learning process—connecting what they already know with what meaning they might perceive in what they are being taught. It creates opportunities for the straightforward practice of new ideas, concepts, and skills to ensure understanding. It also enables the process of applying new information to a different situation, thus ensuring learning transfer. Active learning returns the importance of process to learning. And it does the same thing for returning the role of process to libraries and information use, because it is predicated on the need for students to discover their own experience, skills base, and application strategies for the use of information.

Libraries, Scholarship and Technology (LIS100)

A team of faculty members and librarians developed a semester credit course for information literacy that makes information use and evaluation the centerpiece in the process of producing scholarship. Students learn how scholarship is conducted and created as they discover how different types of information are used for scholarship.

Technology sits in the center of this process of discovery—not as a device for getting information sources but as an environment in which information is presented in a variety of forms. Databases are explored for what they tell the student about the discussion of a topic. Full-text articles are deconstructed to experience how a work of scholarship is constructed, how arguments are created, and how effective refutation is formed. Thus, discourse, the credibility of authors, and the validity of data are three of the key concepts of the course. Technology presents those concepts rather than exclusively acting as a gateway to where those concepts are discussed. Rather than exclusively using a list of articles in a database, retrieved by a keyword subject search, students are asked to discern how that subject has been discussed within the list. This process reveals the various perspectives on the subject that can inform the selection of sources to use.

A technology environment engages students in the process of discovery because of its ability to contain the dynamic that is today's information environment. Today's technology acts as the shelf and journal stack of the pretechnology library. Technology can be viewed as a place, not just as a tool.

Information literacy becomes more than the ability to find a list of sources to choose from. It presents a readily accessible story of how a subject is being explored. Full-text documents are easily available, along with abstracts that summarize the major points of any particular source.

The body of an author's perspective can be easily retrieved with a subsequent search in order to see the development of that author's perspective. Additional key words for topical aspects or related topics can be identified using the text the database provides.

> Information literacy can be understood as a personally defined set of attributes and as a personal perspective on how information is used to give meaning to one's world. Learning, then, is making connections between your internal understanding of yourself in the world and external factors that can

influence that internal world. Information is an external repository of influences. By making this process of connecting the internal to the external deliberate, focused, and efficient, we create our own definition of being a learner and being information literate [Hensley, 2003].

Education can also be viewed as a process by which information is imparted in order to assist in the creation of meaning for an individual in the world. Therefore, an information-literate person is an educated person, and the integration of information literacy into the curriculum of higher education becomes a necessity. The two experiences are intertwined, making each a part of the same experience.

An educated person understands how his or her own perspective is formed and that it is one of many that are possible. Those perspectives can span time and place. Information literacy builds the ability to find those perspectives. Technology provides the avenue to place perspectives in context. A student who plays the ukulele because she wants to, and because it is a part of her own personal and family context, can discover not only the history of the instrument but also the development of the instrument as a habitual aspect of the culture of which she is a member. The result is a more thorough understanding and appreciation for her own skills and why those skills are significant. The question What is this? is transformed into the question How do I connect to this? Meaning is created.

Technology works best when it is used not as a device to get to some place but, rather, as the destination itself. Technology as a destination is not the only environment for learning, but it is effective as a learning environment when it is applied to the process of learning as the learning place. The technology-rich library and the pretechnology library can be the same rich environment for learning. Both environments emphasize exploration and inquiry as necessary pathways to knowing. The student who finds the book section on child abuse must examine and consider the options in order to select the relevant sources. The student needs to do the same thing when presented with forty articles about child abuse from a database or five thousand hits from an Internet search. The criteria for that consideration need to be formed from the meaning the student creates for his or her understanding of child abuse. When students realize that they are responsible for meaning creation, the personal becomes an integral aspect of understanding. Thus, the distance in education is shortened while the ramifications of being knowledgeable are heightened. The process becomes the product, a product always subject to change and expansion.

References

Hensley, R. "Travel Essential, Information Literacy and Learning." In M. Watts, *College: We Make the Road by Walking.* Upper Saddle River, N.J.: Pearson Education, Inc., 2003.

Miller, W. "Troubling Myths About On-Line Information." *Chronicle of Higher Education,* Aug. 1, 1997, p. A44.

Stoffle, C., Renaud, R., and Veldof, J. "Choosing Our Futures." *College and Research Libraries,* 1996, 57(3) 213–225.

RANDY BURKE HENSLEY is head of the Public Services Division at the University of Hawaii at Manoa Library and is the 2002 recipient of the Miriam Dudley Instruction Librarian Award from the Association of College and Research Libraries.

Interlude: A Conversation with Kevin Kelly, Editor of *Wired* Magazine

Margit Misangyi Watts

Walking through the streets of San Francisco to the building that houses the offices of *Wired* magazine, I anticipated coming around a corner and seeing it advertise its whereabouts in neon lights. After all, the magazine is known for its nontraditional, eye-catching, if not dizzying, design and layout. Wouldn't you expect it to offer that same image to the public? Well, it doesn't. It took a while for me to find the street address, in small letters, barely visible. Here was this low-rise, nondescript building with no names, no signs, offering no visible reason to think that I had come upon the offices in which I would find the editor, Kevin Kelly. Inside a small foyer, I found a list of the few offices that occupy the building and discovered that *Wired* was to be found a few floors up. After getting permission from a doorman of sorts to enter the elevator, I went up to my appointment.

Well! The elevator doors opened and I faced an enormous concrete wall painted the brightest pink the world has seen, and on this wall was one locked door, with a security voice box next to it. As soon as I stood in view of this box, a receptionist asked me who I was, and then the door was unlocked for my entry. I walked in and found myself in a waiting room that was contiguous with the whole enterprise. Covers of past issues of *Wired* were hung in the room, the posts were painted in bright colors, the walls were striped and color-coded, and you could feel the rush of business all around you. I was excited to have this opportunity to meet with the man who in effect held the key to the success of the magazine, and who, I thought, would embody the new move toward integrating technology into life. My, was I surprised!

Within a few minutes, Kevin Kelly came out to greet me and took me into the back, past the staff cafeteria, which was laden with luscious-looking sandwiches and healthy salads and such, to a room full of old paintings, graphics, and other collectibles. We sat at a table, exchanged pleasantries (since we had only met over electronic mail and on the phone before this), and began our interview.

I decided to plunge right into the central issue of education by referring to an interview he had given recently, entitled "It Takes a Village to Make a Mall." I asked whether he felt the same way about education. Kelly acknowledged that, indeed, it does take a village to raise a child and suggested that in the end one grows up within an extended family, a community of people and ideas. He stated that well-rounded individuals require socialization and that parents are not sufficient for that. Kelly went on to indicate some trends:

> I think one of the trends we are seeing is that we had a fairly social, small-level, community-based education for many, many years and centuries. I think the last couple of hundred years—maybe 150 years—we had a phenomenon we had never seen before that came with the industrial revolution. This was about a mass market, mass democracy, mass products, mass audiences, and mass education, which worked very well for an industrialized society. Things are changing now and we are moving away from that. In the 1970s, the "Me Decade" and the beginning of personal computers, there was a kind of overreaction, with people lunging toward these technologies. But I think what we are now doing is backing off a little bit and realizing that what the network and technology provides us with inside the Web is not so much the fantasies of personal satisfaction or personal gain. What we see in the new telecommunications is that we have an opportunity to explore a social realm that is not as big as mass audiences, or even the entire nation, but bigger than our neighborhood. It really isn't a wholesale isolation of individuals; there are now middle-sized communities of practice of twenty, communities of interest of one hundred, and extended families of ten—smaller than a mass and larger than a person. I think there is great hope there, because I think this is a more natural place for humans to live—the size of a clan or the size of a village. This is not so much what people are calling the global village, though; this is happening at the same time. But this is very much the idea of exploring—or perhaps modernizing—the concept of having a smaller number than everybody and a larger number than one to do things together in a very intense and strong way.

I agreed with Kelly's notion that the smaller than a mass and larger than one theory of how we humans might actually enjoy living was clearly behind the notion of taking a village to raise a child. But I wondered how he felt technology was involved. So many people feel that the new technologies would actually get in the way of this movement. He disagreed.

> I don't see that. Every step I think that we are taking in the Web and on the Internet is showing that the technology is more powerful than we thought. It is more extensive, it's more humanizing, and every step of the way we are showing again how wrong George Orwell was. In fact, one of the things that the Web and the Internet do is that they show really how stupid and undesirable a lot of the kinds of things we associate with technology really are. Things like the monolithic view of technology. What I think is happening is that this metaphor of technology, this iconic image we have, is going to change.

So, I wondered whether this change meant we would move away from being preoccupied by the wires and the machines, the cold hard metal. He suggested that we would definitely move away from what he called the "monolithic, huge, centralized, brutish" image of technology. Kelly understood the future to move away from hardware.

> We will move from cold, hard, metal to something like simple bamboo and writing and other things. From hardware to software. Things like that. And I think we're right now at a point where we are sort of entering this world by carrying images of what technology is—stainless steel gears—and I think our understanding of that is rather infantile. Certainly infantile. This phase of technology is not about test tubes, chemistry, or gears. In fact, it is much broader and includes double-entry bookkeeping, the alphabet, and things like that. Those more tangible technologies, and perhaps more social technologies, [are] where we are headed. There are certain things that come of this. No one has ever warmed to cold hard metal, and so we have this sort of natural resistance to identify ourselves with it. We didn't have this same resistance to the agricultural tools we invented and used. People loved their tools and actually had a passion for them. I think we need to get back to those feelings.

We both agreed that there was a need to go back to feeling a passion and identification with the tools we conceive and that in the end it will be possible to do so. However, Kelly suggested that much of what we are making today is not yet at a level where we can identify with it. I offered my view that perhaps this was because the new technologies are not yet transparent, and they are more difficult to use than, let's say, a hammer. Kelly agreed that technology needs to become more invisible, disappearing from our consciousness. I presented one example of a transparent technology, which is to walk into a room and expect a light switch to be on the wall as you enter. We don't even think about this technology any longer, we just expect it to be there as part of what we do. He continued with this line of thinking, giving an example of motors, saying that motorization has become successful because we have accepted it as part of our culture, our lives, and he hinted that technology would only become as successful when it becomes invisible.

Changing the direction of our conversation, I asked Kelly about his children. He has three young children, and I wondered how he envisioned their future. I told him about my conversation with Howard Rheingold (see the second Interlude in this volume), and his story of making certain his daughter had the opportunity to touch real trees before they disappeared from our world. I asked Kelly what his reaction to this might be.

> He's wrong, of course. Because there will always be real trees. This is because of the force of life being so much stronger than the forces of nonlife. I'm not sure whether the stronger forces of life lie in our own imaginations or in life itself. But perhaps there isn't much difference. Our minds are the extensions of the forces of life. I think he's right, though, about introducing kids to the

organic, to "treeness." That's a tremendous thing, and Howard has a great passion for this. I think perhaps where we disagree is about the importance of computers over trees. I don't think computers will ever take over the value of trees; [trees] are too important to us. And even if we devoted every single person in America to the eradication of trees, we couldn't do it. Why? Because of this force of life.

After another fifteen minutes of discussing the philosophical implications of what Kelly was suggesting, I turned our conversation to virtual communities. Because many concerns about the new computer technologies stem from a feeling that people will become too attached to these virtual places, I asked if he thought we would really lose touch with reality—whatever reality is. Some think of online environments as unreal places and have come to use an acronym—IRL (in real life). I prefer to use IPL (in physical life) because I do consider my time in virtual environments to be real. However, many are concerned that we might be losing our humanity. I wondered how Kelly felt about this.

I'm actually very much for virtual reality. I think most of the early great things in life have been discovered by folks who are up all night and not sleeping and are directing all their passion [toward] one idea. Now, if a person never ever comes back from this place of contemplation and energy, then that's a problem. But out of intense concentration comes great stuff! And I would hate to see it be otherwise. It is really interesting to read early history—about when the first novels came about. There was terrible moaning and groaning—and high-horsed comments—about how dreadful this escapism was for people. Good citizens and young people spending hours and hours involved in these imaginary worlds with unrealistic situations. These were virtual realities. So now, what we are doing is saying, spend time reading novels instead of being online! There are two things to realize. First of all, there is a great deal of obsessing that is done by young people. That's a phase. Secondly, cultural obsession with technology is also often an adolescent thing. We move from obsession to obsession. We always like to find an avenue of escapism.

Given that we agreed that escapism was going to be a part of human life, be it losing oneself in a novel or immersing oneself in an online environment, I pondered what this meant for decisions affecting educational practice. Do we push books? Do we buy more computers? How do we resolve the need for a varied educational system to cope with the multitude of learning styles? I wondered if the new technologies would help or hinder our need for reform and renewal. Kelly was clear about where he stood in regard to these questions.

Certainly, many people are questioning if computers are a waste of time in school. My own advice to the school that my girls go to is that if they have to spend money that hurts, computers are not necessarily the way to go. And it's not that computers are necessarily destabilizing or contrary to educational values. I just think they are not a very good buy right now. I think they are basically too expensive. If they were only twenty dollars, like a textbook, then you could have one for every student, which is as it should be. Until we can do that, they are not really valuable. If [they] have a lot of money, discretionary income, and price is not an issue, then they should have them. And generally it is the parents who supply them. That's what we've done. Of course, this is for other reasons, not necessarily economic ones. [My children] just have my old ones. So they've never learned computers, but they use them all the time. I would certainly not suggest that schools take monies from the library or science lab to buy computers. I don't think that's a very good thing to do right now.

Agreeing with Kelly, I noted that we see art and music departments being closed all over the country; yet these same schools are laying out large amounts of money for new computer labs. Kelly was convinced that this was not a good trend, even though he believes that children should have access to computers. Because of the expense of technology, he finds us in a situation that forces us to really evaluate our choices. He continues talking about his own children.

I have very conditional ideas about lower elementary grades. We have our children in a fairly traditional setting which addresses character and values, the importance of learning, [and] fundamental things, [and] I actually think that if you apply rote and drill, it will foster an attitude about learning that will continue on. Also, the other thing that we personally discovered is that there is no perfect school, and all you have to do is find a school in which the parents, family, and community come together and compensate for whatever you are missing. We are pretty creative and have come up with some pretty interesting stuff as a family. So what we have decided is, we would take the basic traditional education and then compensate with our own family activities. This is versus having a very creative free-forming school situation for our children. But this is my personal preference, to have the traditional foundation for my children.

I was delighted to hear that his family and the community in which Kelly chose to raise his children would indeed compensate for whatever shortcomings one would find in the schools there. But, I queried, what about the rest of the world? What should we suggest to others? He was adamant that we needed to get around the idea of mass education. He recommended a voucher system and felt that it would go a long way toward liberating educational practice and [would] create a possibility for change, as well as introduce a real competition of ideas. Kelly was also quite clear that other changes had to occur. He suggested that teachers should be treated as professionals, they should work all year, have a telephone in their classrooms, and, optimally, be paid as professionals. Everything else, in his way of thinking, would fall into place. This would mean the curriculum and such. He felt that at present we have a very ancient system, still tied to our industrial selves. I wondered, as our conversation was nearing the end, if he could see the role technology would play in all of this. He and I agreed that it wouldn't go away and that we were not going to escape modern technology, and the sooner we left the industrialized mentality that was prevalent, the better would be how we "school" our children. He was, however, cautious, and he told this story:

> I went to Silicon Valley a while back and visited a modified Montessori kind of school. It was very progressive and innovative, and in some sense [it was] sort of horrifying because each kid had their own little cubicle, their own personal computer, desk, chair, whatever. And every morning they would start the day with a kind of game where they would all meet and talk about what they were going to do. It was almost like having your staff meeting in the morning. Many parallels could be found. It was startling to me, and even though I am certain we cannot ignore the new computer technologies and the influences these will and do have on our lives, I'm pretty sure this wasn't the way to go.

I smiled at his story, imagining all of those little Dilberts in their cubicles, and then in the friendly banter and chatter of the last minutes of our conversation I found that Kelly didn't own a television, didn't carry a cell phone, was not nearly as "wired" as I might have guessed. So much for the new tools! And thus, I left with as much surprise as when I first came upon the unpretentious building in the middle of San Francisco.

4

This chapter discusses what technology will not do for higher education and also what it has the potential to provide.

No Magic Answers

Barry M. Maid

Technology, especially the world of networked computers, is responsible for many amazing changes. Yet perhaps the world of "high tech, emerging technologies" is responsible for no greater transformation than the one that ordinarily levelheaded and pragmatic academic administrators, business people, legislators, and members of governing boards undergo. Just the mention of using new technologies in the classroom and, especially, using them for distance education pushes these groups into visions of fantasy. It almost appears as though technology acts as a mind-altering drug for otherwise staid and responsible individuals.

If this vision of having computer technology save the world were isolated, and if only one group would have fantastic visions, we might ascribe it to a variety of local issues. Yet the fantasy is widespread—almost universal in American higher education as we move ahead in the twenty-first century. Surely, there must be common, underlying reasons for so many to want to be swept away. I think if we take a close look at the present state of the American academy, we can find an interesting constellation of reasons why so many leaders turn into starry-eyed idealists when they talk about technology.

Finding many problems with higher education in the United States is easy. However, in order to understand higher education's current fascination and obsession with technology, I think we can isolate three large issues: (1) a general lack of connection from the rest of society, (2) the inability to respond quickly, and (3) gross underfunding.

No Connection

The separation of the academy from the rest of the world is not new. The roots of the separation lie at the very heart of the medieval origin of the university. Yet life in the twenty-first century is very different from life in the fourteenth century. I think no one will argue that the university should be like the rest of society, but it can no longer function in relatively complete isolation. Indeed, for the most part, even our students are no longer cut off from the rest of society. For more and more of them, academic life is just one piece of a greater whole. Many students juggle career and family responsibilities, along with academic pressures. Faculty have always lived in both worlds, though they may be less willing to admit to it. For many faculty, the life of the mind, especially as it leads to print, is all that matters. Ernest Boyer's critique of the American professoriate (1990), though now ten years old, still rings very true. While some might quibble with Boyer's taxonomy, the issues he identifies are still part of an ongoing discussion on most campuses.

Slow, Oh So Slow

Sometimes I suspect that the favorite fable of those in higher education is that of the tortoise and the hare. If nothing else, it gives justification for the academy's propensity to brainstorm, plan, strategize, propose, study, debate, revise, and so forth—in other words, to do everything but act. In a world when long-distance communication took days, weeks, or more, perhaps the slow, thoughtful, reflective process that academics seem to cherish so made sense. Now, as we live in a society where worldwide telecommunications are measured in fractions of seconds, any slow process seems woefully outdated, or even worse, simply inadequate. Although I would not argue that academics need to reject thoughtful reflection for the sake of speed alone, I would suggest that when it takes an institution three to five years to consider and adopt a change, and then another three to five years to implement that change, the institution is wasting its time and resources. Using that time frame, the change is most likely outdated before it will be approved— and long before it can be implemented.

Inadequate Funding

If the first two problems are internal ones and therefore something those in the academy might have some control over, the last problem is external and is even more frustrating because those in higher education have little control over it. Although no one wants to hear that any governmental entity needs more money, simply denying a reality does not make it go away. The sad fact is that in many instances those in higher education have done too good a job of making do with little or nothing. The public, and especially too many legislators, see that every time higher education has been called on to do more with less, they have stepped up and responded. The feeling is, then, that still more "fat" exists out there. Of course, a close examination of how higher education has managed is insightful. Sam Walton was not the only CEO to implement a system of hiring only part-time workers at a low wage and denying them benefits. American universities have been operating on the same model for years. This is not the place to discuss the merits and problems of adjunct faculty; however, the reality is that most institutions would have to make serious cutbacks in the number of courses they offer if courses were taught only by full-time faculty.

The Magic Answer

So, given the three problems of a lack of connection to the rest of the world, the inability to move in a timely fashion, and the endemic lack of funding and technology—especially networked computers—seems to indicate the magic answer. I think a close analysis of what technology might offer higher education will reveal some interesting possibilities. However, it will also reveal some serious limitations. I can therefore understand the optimism surrounding the insertion and integration of technology into higher education. What I must admit to having trouble understanding is how otherwise levelheaded pragmatists can honestly believe that there will be magic answers for the real problems I've just defined.

The Distance Myth

In 1999, I happened to attend the 15th Annual Conference on Distance Teaching and Learning, held at the University of Wisconsin–Madison. Though having used computers in my classroom teaching since the mid-1980s, and having taught in both networked computing and interactive video environments since the early 1990s, I had my eyes opened. I was clearly out of my league. I went as a faculty member who had experience and, I hope, some expertise in using technology to deliver classes. In addition, I have served as a very low-level administrator. I ran a writing program and had been a department chair. The main audience at the conference were the deans of continuing education, provosts, and presidents. The vendors I was used to dealing with sold textbooks or software at prices I understood. The vendors here sold products that easily cost ten times my department's entire yearly operating budget. Although not in a position of institutional power, unlike most of the other attendees, I still listened to the speakers and talked to the exhibitors. I came away convinced that the conference this particular year was one where the greedy were preaching to the ignorant.

I heard speakers talk about the possibility of sharing digital copies of documents, musical recordings, and videos in what I would now call "Napster-like" terms. There was never a mention of copyright or intellectual property rights. Digitization was simply going to save money. Likewise, I heard people talk about how computer technology would enable one faculty member to teach hundreds, perhaps thousands, of students at a time. The model, of course, was a simply webbed lecture note and machine-scored multiple-choice exam. It was as though the Internet had become the educational Philosopher's Stone, turning base metal correspondence courses into educational gold. Interestingly, no one bothered to mention that students who pay their own money for courses are not very likely to pay for a course like that more than once.

Finally, while talking with some of the exhibitors about the high bandwidth necessary to use their products, I was quickly informed that bandwidth was not a problem. They were happy to inform me that the overwhelming majority of students who sign up for these classes are regularly enrolled students living in campus housing with high-speed Internet connections in their rooms. Apparently, unlike most of the other attendees, I questioned the use of limited resources to develop classes so that on-campus students wouldn't have to get up for 8:00 A.M. classes.

So Technology's Not the Answer for. . . .

As a result of all the promise and hype, and the difficulty in separating the two, I think before we can look at what technology can do for us, we need to seriously address what it cannot do. I have tried to start. First of all, technology will not solve our money problems. In most instances, I suspect it will cost more than it will bring in. Interestingly enough, though, I suspect that if used wisely and effectively in the delivery of distance learning courses, technology might, over time, make money. Although it is unlikely that technology will ever be the cash cow people are promising, it may still be profitable. The important thing here is the phrase *over time*.

If It Won't Make Us Rich, Why Should We Bother?

I do think there are many good reasons to use technology in the classroom. I also think that there are many good reasons to explore the possibilities of new technologies in distance learning classes. In fact, if my feelings were not so strong about it, I suspect I would be less bothered by what I see as the faulty and inadequate uses of technology. From my perspective, we would be much better served if we looked at how the use of technology in the classroom can benefit both our students and us.

Right now, I think the single most important reason we integrate technology into our classes is that we have no choice. Our students, our society, and our culture demand it. To not do so is to not give our students the best education we can. Using technology is now the normal way of doing business outside the academy. If we choose to remain disconnected, as we have in the past, we will be cheating our students. I think we can begin to understand just how pervasive technology has become outside the academy by looking at anecdotal evidence from my own teaching experience. I first started requiring that students use e-mail for classes in the early nineties. Back then, I needed to negotiate with my institution to make sure all my students had e-mail accounts, and I then had to train the students in how to use e-mail. Things have changed. Now, my opening class discussions about e-mail are not about what it is and how to use it but, rather, which account should students use (their university account, their ISP account, their work account, or an anonymous account). For those who complain that using technology in the classroom draws away from teaching the class subject matter to teaching the technology, I can only say that this example shows that it runs full circle. In the beginning, I did need to use class time to teach the technology. Now, however, the discussion about the technology (which address to use) is clearly a discussion in establishing the ethos.

Local institutional conditions might drive some institutions toward creative uses of technology that may or may not be appropriate elsewhere. In an attempt to help a situation of classroom overcrowding, the freshman composition program at Utah State University went online. Christine Hult and David Hailey (2000) report that when they "tried to conduct the classes entirely through the virtual environment, many students got lost or frustrated and dropped the online course." They conclude that "the need for meeting face-to-face seems to be dependent on the group of learners in the course. In our graduate online courses in technical writing, students never meet face-to-face, and this group of learners seems able to cope better without the in-person teacher direction that the freshmen seem to need. It only makes sense that graduate students, as a group, would typically be more independent learners."

Using technology in order to offer completely online classes, or even hybrids, can help schools where classroom space is an issue.

Finally, It's About Teaching

Most of us who teach in universities receive no training as teachers. We learn a subject that we then are expected to teach. As a result, our initial efforts are usually simply attempts to replicate the teaching methods we observed as students. In most instances, we have two defaults: if we teach a large class, we lecture, and if we teach a small class, we lecture and hold discussions. However, once teachers start to use technology in their classes, especially when they use networked computers, some interesting issues arise. The first thing most teachers notice is that the online version of the lecture method does not work very well. (Actually, some might even suggest that it also fails to work in face-to-face environments.) In fact, when teachers start looking at the methods they use while teaching in electronic environments, they discover that every virtual environment is different. The Web is different from text only. Synchronous is different from asynchronous. Video (and, yes, video that is both interactive and streamed is virtual) is different from the Web. What this means is, instructors who find themselves teaching in a variety of media find themselves rethinking and reshaping their pedagogy, based on the medium they are working in. Even more interesting is that there seems to be transference back to face-to-face instruction. In much the same way that faculty who have worked in writing centers talk about a change in the way they teach in the classroom as a result of their writing center experiences, faculty who teach in virtual environments become more sensitive to their teaching in face-to-face classes. If the only thing that infusing technology into the classroom accomplished was to make faculty members more sensitive to and thoughtful about how they teach, I'd suggest it as a good enough reason to argue for technology.

And, Finally, What Do We Do About Courseware?

Most campuses now encourage faculty who use technology in their classes, both locally and at a distance, to use whatever large course management software package the campus has purchased—usually either WebCT or Blackboard. I suspect nothing is inherently evil in wanting some way to let faculty who are not technologically advanced be able to quickly put some of their coursework online. In fact, the large courseware packages can give faculty members a variety of useful tools at their fingertips—when those tools work. Faculty experienced in teaching with technology can usually decide what part of the courseware to use and what part to work around. The biggest problem I see with these large packages are not the modules that will work only in future versions or the security issues. All those are issues that should eventually be worked out. The problem is that the software seems to be constructed around a particular kind of pedagogy—the virtual equivalent of the large lecture hall, where students listen, take notes, and are then tested, using multiple-choice tests.

I expect the reason for this is the same reason that many faculty members choose to use this method in their face-to-face classes. This teaching method is easier for the faculty: post your lecture notes to the Web, have your students enter a secure portion of the site, and take a multiple-choice exam, which is immediately scored by the computer, with results given instantly to the student and recorded in the instructor's gradebook. Unfortunately, this kind of teaching, which is rarely effective face-to-face, seems to be even less effective online. Yet this is exactly the default pedagogy for large courseware packages. Of course, experienced faculty can do other things. Novice users can be trained to do other things, as well, but if the training is thorough and effective, it brings them to a point beyond where the courseware may be useful. Like all technologies, courseware should be used only when its use somehow enhances or widens the educational experience. We use technology in order to reach students who might not otherwise be reached—whether because of distance, time conflicts, or learning styles, or for any other possible reasons. Bringing technology into classes has the potential effect of opening up learning opportunities for students that might not otherwise exist. At the base of these new learning opportunities is the assumption that students are at the center of their own education. So, by using a classroom technology such as PowerPoint, we might engage visual learners more readily. By using a threaded discussion board, we might enable the student who hadn't completely formulated a question or a response in the designated fifty-minute period to become a full participant in the class.

So What Does It All Mean?

If I had real answers, I suspect I would be on the lecture and talk show tour. Since all I do is write small chapters in books, I can only make some suggestions. We in higher education need to embrace technology because it is a social and cultural norm. More important, it may provide us with one of the most powerful tools to allow us to look closely at how we teach in order to become more effective teachers, no matter what medium we may be working in. Still, we must remain diligent about technology's ability to standardize and be careful that it does not lure us into what can only be called "one-size fits all" education. When people tout the one size fits all model, they usually leave off, from the end of the phrase, the word *badly*. Perhaps the question we need to ask is, Does the use of this technology specifically benefit the institution, or is it likely to enhance student learning? Clearly, we might find instances in which some technologies might do both. However, if there is ever a question about the use of technology, we must always err on the side of the student. Finally, we must resist the belief that technology will provide an easy and magic answer for all our ills.

References

Boyer, E. *Scholarship Reconsidered: Priorities of the Professoriate.* Princeton, N.J.: Carnegie Foundation for the Advancement of Teaching, 1990.

Hult, C., and Hailey, D. "Virtual English at Utah State University." *Computers and Composition,* 2000. [http://corax.cwrl.utexas.edu/cac/online/00/hult_hailey/ Intro_T. htm].

BARRY M. MAID is professor and head faculty member of technical communication at Arizona State University East.

5

This chapter is a personal account of the transformative nature of technology on the teaching and learning of one faculty member.

A MOOcentric Perspective on Education and Information Technology

Wesley Cooper

As an old goat who roamed the Internet long before Al Gore had reason to dub it the Information Superhighway, I am both an early adopter of this new technology and a first-generation immigrant to it. Unlike contemporary college students, I had to make adjustments to a mature adult sensibility, my own, that had been molded by the book and by educational institutions that were innocent about information technology. Although they, too, are immigrants to cyberspace, our students have done their traveling at an early age, with relatively little cultural baggage. So I regard them as subsequent-generation immigrants. I am issei, so to speak; they are nisei or sansei.

While on sabbatical leave in Montreal in 1983, I acquired my first computer, a Sanyo PC clone running DOS and featuring the word processing program WordStar. Brought up by parents who had been seared by the Depression, I was too much of a cheapskate to buy up to the Apple Macintosh, which had begun the personal computer revolution in the mid-seventies and was just beginning to lose ground to the IBM PC with its Microsoft-owned operating system—fatefully licensed, but not bought, by IBM. Like everyone else I know, I never looked back to writing with a typewriter, not to mention pen and paper. The centuries-old brain-hand-writing implement-paper connection had been quickly displaced by the new brain-hand-ASCII-wired keyboard-computer file sequence. Subsequently, I learned to interact with a mainframe from a dumb terminal, accessing the mainframe's printing facilities, not to mention its delightful single-user adventure games.

New Directions for Teaching and Learning, no. 94, Summer 2003 © Wiley Periodicals, Inc.

In 1989, two friends of mine, doctoral students in my department, returned from a conference in Vancouver, British Columbia, where they met others who told them about multiuser adventure games that were accessible from our dumb terminals. They brought with them an IP address—a series of numbers uniquely designating some computer out there—for a MUD. Subsequently, I learned that this acronym was for Multi-User Dungeon, and that the series of numbers was a ticket to ride the Internet. The MUD was a riotous carnival called Mud Dog, and its server was located somewhere a continent away (in Florida, in fact). I gave my character there the name Mirror, and I declared that the gender was female. This gender bending proved to be a big mistake, because, contrary to what I expected, they took gender seriously in cyberspace. I moved on to a MUD called HoloMUCK, where I named myself Fang and described myself as a wolf's paw. HoloMUCK was interesting because it made an internal programming language available to its users. I began to learn programming there in a multiuser version of the language FORTH. Then I discovered LambdaMOO and its relatively easy-to-learn language, MOO, and my skill as a MUD programmer blossomed. By 1994, I felt able to set up my own MUD at the University of Alberta, and I began experimenting with it as an educational environment. I now call myself DrC on Alberta MOO and describe myself as a "philosophy professor who moonlights here as a wizard."

The problem is that such MUDs as mine were not user-friendly. They were "textual realities," relying entirely on the imaginations of their users and their manipulations of many arcane commands. Although you could rely on some students taking to it as ducks to water, many more would sink like stones, needing the colors, images, and hyperlinks that began to dominate the Internet after the mid-nineties, which make up the so-called World-Wide Web. By the beginning of the new century, MOO programmers had figured out how to integrate MOO and WWW. I adopted one of these, the enCore database, which adds a computational layer on top of the LambdaMOO source code and database core, gluing the Web's language—HTML—into MOO programs ("verbs"). The result is definitely a hack—to use a term that has both pejorative and laudatory connotations, and it works! I have used the hack as Alberta MOO for several academic years now, with increasing success. The increase is a complex function of the integrative technology, my growing understanding of it as reflected in my programming for my courses and my sense for what will work for the classes I'm teaching, and the year-after-year rise in my students' competence with integrative technology (IT).

Another integration should be mentioned—that between traditional educational practice and distance education. For I am not reporting about, or making a case for, pure distance education. I know very little about that. The je ne sais quoi of physical particularity in appearance, voice, and so forth is indispensable to my conception of education, and I am not holding my breath while the Internet learns how to duplicate these. (Nor am I betting against the duplication, or an adequate approximation thereto, in the long haul. Consider the source, however: I've been a trekkie since William Shatner commanded the bridge of the Enterprise. I can make perfect sense of the holodeck.) But the particularity of students and teacher, and of the four walls and the blackboard and chalk, are now being integrated with IT, and that is what I know something about and recommend with growing enthusiasm as a "middle way" between the extremes of pure traditional education on one hand and pure distance education on the other hand.

This Aristotelian golden mean undercuts any critique of IT-mediated education that assumes Either/Or. The argument that the values of an education in the liberal arts require the traditional university rather than distance education technologies of the Internet is footless against the integrative approach illustrated by Alberta MOO. Even granting that the requirement is absolute counts nothing against the thought that integrating IT into the Four Walls enhances education. That can take two forms: first, the use of IT in the classroom, and second, the use of IT in the students' and teachers' own time, at home or in the office or computer lab. I've found the second form more important by far. The classroom is designed for human interaction, which can easily be subverted by reliance on IT technique—unless it's used deftly and subtly. But time outside the classroom is an underexploited resource. We pay lip service to it with the gesture of "office hours," but students don't make much use of them, especially at institutions such as large universities, where access to faculty offices tends to be a time-consuming hassle. It's significant, too, that the practice of office hours puts the whole burden on the student to show up, while the teacher sits in the office, perhaps hoping that his research won't be interrupted.

The integrative approach overcomes the office hours syndrome, and it also adds bells and whistles that won't be found in the office. For instance, my students make great use of VASE, the Virtual Assignment Server Environment in Alberta MOO's enCore database. They write personal sketches, essays, and take-home examinations on VASE. The instructor has the scope to configure assignments to his specifications, and he is allowed to write and send comments and inform the students that the comments are available for viewing. To take another instance, we use MOOmail not only for personal correspondence but also, more important, for participating in mailing lists, especially a list for the discussion of course issues. I have contributed a quiz that combines the textual dexterity of the MOO with the colors and images of the Web, permitting me to create engaging quizzes quickly with explanations as well as answers. These are available whenever the student has the time to enter the MOO and take the quiz. Another of my programs is a voting booth, which gets used once or twice a term to resolve some contentious issues. And there are several other programs, such as one that remembers birthdays and tells horoscopes, that are just fun. Isn't that all right?

Neither VASE nor MOOmail nor my little programs are unique educational tools, of course. I cite them as reminders of groups of tools, some of which, like e-mail, are by now ubiquitous features of the social landscape. So although my perspective on education and information technology is MOOcentric, it draws attention to an integrative model that is not. Being representative of such groups, my reminders show how IT has integrated with culture—a rebuttal in itself of the Either/Or critique of distance education. It's not that the Internet is replacing the traditional classroom; rather, the Internet is remedying certain deficiencies in the traditional classroom, such as students' liability to passivity and boredom, while respecting its time-tested value. This doesn't necessarily mean that every teacher should use IT; much less does it mean that everyone should use MOO. As the Internet acronym has it, YMMV (your mileage may vary).

I spend more time on teaching than I used to, and this is traceable in part to my use of IT. However, I suspect that all teachers spend more time on their work than in decades past, whatever their teaching style, because expectations have risen. Also, I find that IT introduces efficiencies that save time and effort in mechanical tasks such as recording grades, collecting and distributing essays, and administering tests—freeing up more class time for teaching as well as more out-of-class time for commenting on papers. It helps to enjoy the technology. In the old days, I would quickly grow weary of writing out comments by hand on student papers, whereas the crisp efficiency of the VASE protocol for comments keeps me fresh and interested much longer.

A colleague once told me that he would begin using a computer when someone showed him that Martin Heidegger used one. He was making two points: For one thing, Heidegger wrote a lot of books, so it's not as though one needs a computer to be a prolific writer. And my colleague's other—more questionable—point was an allusion to Heidegger's influential philosophy of technology, which lambastes high technology for its role in molding the culture of modernity, specifically furthering a manipulative mind-set toward nature and other people. But this is not the place for an extended discussion of Heidegger's dystopian philosophy of technology and its many imitators in the contemporary academic press. Instead, I will rehearse one or two modest but sturdy facts that don't consort well with that philosophy. As was just mentioned, I use less class time for mechanical tasks and more of it for philosophical interaction with my students, contrary to the hypothesis that IT would lead the teacher in the direction of treating students like cattle on a factory farm. Also, I know my students and how their minds work better than I once did, because of VASE's commenting protocol and the permanent record it affords, as well as MOOmail communication on course matters. This may or may not be a point in favor of pure distance education; I leave that to educators who defend such a model. I am advancing my modest-but-sturdy facts as figuring in an integrative (impure) model in which IT is an adjunct to the traditional classroom, against negative Heideggerian expectations.

My neo-Luddite colleague retired long ago and died recently, leaving one less soul in the "old country" of the intellectual Amish. These people cling to an experiment in living with fewer and fewer adherents. That in itself is a kind of refutation, especially to the degree that those who have migrated to IT have done so freely and rationally. (I see no reason to impugn them—us— on this score.) Still, one should be glad that these experiments have any adherents at all, in order that they might afford vivid illustrations of alternative ways of living. One wouldn't object to Theodore Kaczynski if he'd merely retreated to a commune that practiced his vision of utopia, mailing out disgruntled letters to the *New York Times* now and then. What's objectionable in the intellectual echoes of the Unabomber's physical coercion is the conceit that we must lead technology-free lives—the "must" being a sign of an attempt at intellectual coercion. It is sometimes masked by a political philosophy of communitarianism, which criticizes liberal tolerance on the grounds that we should all participate in the same conception of the good. Kaczynski's example explains why Thomas Nagel concludes an essay (1998) by writing, "Communitarianism—the ambition of collective self-realization— is one of the most persistent threats to the human spirit."

Earlier, I mentioned my initial surprise that gender matters in something as abstract and computational as cyberspace. I now think that my reaction reflects the dualism I have been criticizing—that between traditional values and the new information technology. Given the dualism, it's reasonable to adopt a hostile posture toward IT in education. I have challenged the dualism by defending a mixed, integrative model in which IT is an adjunct to the traditional classroom. This dualism is implicit in an otherwise charming image that is my favorite recollection of resisting the Vietnam War so long ago: a photograph of my peers putting flowers down the barrels of rifles held by national guardsmen. The photo seems to say, "You deal in high-tech weapons and death, whereas we represent love and nature." The flowers negate the technology. A more adequate, less dualistic image would show the flowers transforming the rifles into amazing flower-projecting devices, good to turn deserts into gardens. Something like this has happened on the Internet, where MUDs and IRC were in the low-bandwidth vanguard, followed later by the high-bandwidth images, sounds, and virtual realities of the Web. They have transformed the computer as calculating machine—zeroes and ones on mathematical parade, good to make John von Neumann's calculations about implosion in atomic bombs into a medium of communication, expression, and representation. Educational values are one aspect of that transformation.

Reference

Nagel, T. "Concealment and Exposure." 1998. [http://www.nyu.edu/gsas/dept/philo/faculty/nagel].

WESLEY COOPER is a professor of philosophy at the University of Alberta. He is the author, recently, of The Unity of William James's Thought.

A case study of creating community through distance learning is examined, focusing on the use of low-cost technology to link students across six time zones, the interdisciplinary approaches used, and the implications for national and global community building.

A Case Study: Linking Students Across Geographical and Cultural Distances

Stephen J. Romanoff

This case study examines how technology-based distance learning can enhance learning and teaching, as well as foster a broader sense of community between students separated by great distances. An abiding concern among teachers and administrators about distance learning is how it excludes or diminishes the face-to-face human contact inherent in a conventional classroom (Cho and Berg, 2002). Parks and Floyd (1996) examine the contrasting positions concerning online relationships in Internet newsgroups, particularly how some scholars view these relationships as "shallow, impersonal, and often hostile," seeing that "only the illusion of community can be created in cyberspace" (p. 1). Parks and Floyd also acknowledge the support lent to distance learning by some of its champions: "On the other side are those who argue that computer-mediated communications liberates interpersonal relations from the confines of physical locality and thus creates opportunities for new, but genuine, personal relationships and communities."

Perhaps nowhere is that human contact more present than in undergraduate learning communities (Astin, 1993, 1996; Tussman, 1969). One of the most compelling features of learning communities is that they effectively bring students and teachers together into more intimate groups (Shapiro and Levine, 1999). It was, therefore, ironic that Temple University's Learning Community electronic-mail listserv introduced me to Margit Watts, with whom I collaborated in creating a long-distance, virtual learning community between students in Maine and Hawaii.

The term *distance education* suggests physical distance between faculty members and some or all of their students (University System of Maryland,

1997). One of this project's unique features was that primary faculty members remained physically present with their students while the two primary collaborating student groups were physically separated by nearly six thousand miles. This was not a conventional "eCourse," with one or more teachers delivering instructional material over a closed-circuit television screen. Rather, it was a course taught concurrently in Maine and Hawaii by in-house instructors to groups of students who were collaborating with their distant counterparts on similar assignments via e-mail and the chat room.

Real-time interaction between all participating students, faculty, school administrators, and museum administrators was an attractive, though challenging, variable for the project. Through the use of e-mail and a MOO chat room, all participants were, in theory, able to interact in real time, notwithstanding the obstacles inherent in computer-dependent communication. For example, a substantial portion of student and faculty collaboration took place by e-mail, some of which was often not retrieved or answered in real time. Steiner (1995) describes synchronous instruction as a delivery system of distance education that requires the simultaneous participation of all students and instructors. Asynchronous instruction employs less than simultaneous participation. Steiner's report uses the terms collaboration and instruction interchangeably, because students, faculty, and administrators were continually exchanging ideas on subject, design, implementation, and evaluation. Subsequently, both synchronous and asynchronous instructional delivery systems were in play during most of the phases of this project.

Project Abstract

During the winter and spring of 1999, participants in the Russell Scholars Program (RSP) of the University of Southern Maine in Gorham and the Rainbow Advantage Program (RAP) of the University of Hawaii at Manoa collaborated on a traveling art exhibit entitled "Celebrations: Windows Into Culture." The goal of the project was to create a larger learning community from several smaller communities that are physically, and to some extent culturally, separated by great distances, through the use of creative arts and humanities curricula and the available technology of electronic mail and a multidimensional chat room. Other participants in the project were fifth and sixth graders from the Gorham Village School in Maine, third and fifth graders from Le Jardin Academy in Honolulu, and eighth graders from Iolani School in Honolulu, as well as staff at the Portland Museum of Art in Maine and the Bishop Museum in Honolulu.

Members of the Maine and Hawaii learning communities conferred by e-mail or the chat room on every aspect of the project, with the objective of sharing both the experience of researching creating the art works and actually sharing the exhibits. Maine would ship its project to Hawaii for a concurrent exhibit, and the Hawaii and Maine projects would return together to Maine for a concurrent exhibit.

The Learning Community

Alexander Meiklejohn (1932) defines a learning community as a specific cohort of students and faculty for whom the curriculum is deliberately restructured in order to meet their educational objectives. The learning community concept is a traditional format that has been effectively employed for centuries, first in European universities and then in North American universities. Today's learning communities emphasize the reduction of impediments to effective teaching by designing "any one of a variety of curricular structures that link together several existing courses. . . . so that students have opportunities for deeper understanding and integration of the material they are learning, and more interaction with one another and their teachers as fellow participants in the learning enterprise" (Gabelnick, McGregor, Matthews, and Smith, 1990, p. 5).

Learning communities are present in formats such as freshman interest groups or FIGS (Tinto, Goodsell-Love, and Russo, 1993), which employ more collaborative teaching and learning through the design of a more interdisciplinary linkage (Levine and Tompkins, 1996). The primary benefits of effective learning communities are that they

- Create smaller units of students
- Encourage integration of the curriculum
- Establish academic and social support networks
- Provide a setting for students to become socialized as college students
- Help students deal with feelings of anonymity and detachment experienced in larger classes
- Bring faculty together
- Focus faculty and students on learning outcomes
- Provide a base for community-based delivery of student support services
- Serve as a critical lens for examining undergraduate education, particularly the first-year experience (Shapiro and Levine, 1999)

Studies have demonstrated that students in learning communities tend to have higher grades, attend more classes, be more engaged in campus activities, have greater satisfaction with their collegiate experience, and remain enrolled at the institution (Johnson and Romanoff, 1999; Tinto, Goodsell-Love, and Russo, 1993).

Russell Scholars Program

The Russell Scholars Program (RSP) is a residential interdisciplinary learning community at the University of Southern Maine (USM), offering traditional students team-taught-linked courses that satisfy some core requirements. First-year RSP students live in the same residence hall, whose first floor is dedicated to RSP classrooms and faculty offices. The program serves good-to-excellent students with a commitment to collaborative learning, critical thinking, global learning, and service learning during their four to five years at USM ("Russell Scholars at USM," 2002). A rich co-curriculum, along with regular mentoring, has contributed higher retention, a higher grade point average, and higher student satisfaction than a control group (Johnson and Romanoff, 1999). Students are required to complete twenty-one RSP credits in order to graduate as a Russell Scholar.

Rainbow Advantage Program

The Rainbow Advantage Program (RAP) is a first-year learning community at the University of Hawaii at Manoa that offers general education courses in a supportive environment, promoting a sense of community and shared values. Providing a small college atmosphere within the larger university, RAP is based on the coordinated studies model emphasizing collaborative teaching and learning, challenging students to view knowledge as the development and building of connections. RAP also uses a rich curriculum that engages students outside the classroom. The concept of a global classroom guides the philosophy and activities of RAP, which makes wide use of technology and a variety of links to the wider community. RAP's intensive use of technology and the development of its COllaboratory and Walden3 MOO were indispensable components in the RSP/RAP Project. RAP students take fifteen credits together during their first year, six of which are from a foundation course that teaches research skills and has them ultimately do their own primary research study.

The Technology

RSP students had twenty-four-hour access to four IBM PCs in the RSP computer lab in the residence hall. They also had access to the university's larger computer labs; however, these labs opened at 7:00 A.M. and closed at 11:00 P.M. Most RSP students also had PCs in their rooms, but they were not always powerful enough for Walden3 MOO. The Village School students had difficulty accessing Walden3 from their school; however, many were able to access it from their homes. Most students and teachers were able to subscribe to the COllaboratory listserv, allowing them to communicate with anyone by e-mail. Communicating was often problematic, due to the limitations of multiple Internet servers between Maine and Hawaii.

Virtual Learning Community

Margit Watts, director of RAP, had created two devices: COllaboratory and Walden3 MOO, by which RAP students and their distance learning partners could communicate across great geographical distances. Collaboratory is an initiative within the foundations course of RAP and is a capstone activity of the yearlong course connecting RAP students, K–12 students, museum staff, and other students and faculty from around the country. All the Maine and Hawaii students, faculty, and administrators subscribed to COllaboratory's electronic mail listserv. In addition, everyone subscribed to and logged on to Walden3, a multidimensional real-time chat room. Walden3 is a MOO (MUD Object-Oriented) that provides a text-based platform for word building and synchronous communication, enabling students, faculty, staff, librarians, and museum partners to communicate with each other in real time. The ability to quickly communicate long distance was essential given the time difference and the need to discuss myriad details of the project. The multidimensional feature of Walden3 allowed students to arrange to rendezvous where they could talk privately without interruption. Students would typically log on to the MOO and announce their presence by joining the general discussion, or they would recognize that they were being paged and would then move to that specific room within the MOO to pursue a more private conversation. Several rooms within the MOO could be used for exclusive conversations. Visitors could invite specific guests to join their conversation, and they could exclude others. To our knowledge, this last option was not employed to any extent during the project.

Rationale

Watts's Collaboratory had successfully launched several museum-based projects in the years prior to RSP/RAP. Our collaboration would be the first formal collaboration initiative between two major educational institutions in Maine and Hawaii, and it would also be the first collaboration between art museums in Maine and Hawaii.

The similarities and differences between the participants were compelling. Many RAP students were natives of Hawaii and were of Hawaiian, Pacific, and Asian American heritage, and they had never been to the East Coast or to Maine. Most RSP students were from New England, of Anglo American heritage, and had never been far from New England. Maine and Hawaii each has a rich maritime heritage and each state relies heavily on tourism.

The common denominators between the RSP and RAP students were their shared identity as U.S. citizens and their common age and commercial demographic. They listened to and watched the same popular music, movies, and television, and they shared experiences and issues similar to those of American college students. Likewise, the third, fifth, and eighth graders in the project shared experiences and issues common to their age groups. Watts and I believed that these student similarities, when introduced into a dynamic arts and humanities project, would ultimately forge a community out of strangers and dramatically shorten the distance between these far-flung partners.

Design and Methodology

Watts and I decided to use celebrations as a research vehicle for students to learn about a specific group or culture. We entitled the project "Celebrations: Windows Into Culture" and invited all the participants to discuss specifications and materials. We decided on twelve-foot-high decorated fabric hangings, twenty-eight inches in width. Each hanging was dedicated to one celebration from anywhere in the world. Faculty from the universities and public schools agreed that a combination of small-group and large-group instruction would be most effective. Third and fifth graders visited the RSP students at USM to discuss the project and to go online with Hawaii's RAP students on USM's computers. Student teams selected and reserved the celebration they wished to research and represent with their hangings. The commonality between students became dramatically clear when students on both sides of the country realized that they were often competing for the same topic to research and explicate. This minor problem served to illustrate to all parties how the distance between them was already diminishing. Examples of some selected celebrations were Kwanza, Makahiki, Samoan Flag Day, Veterans Day, Guy Fawkes Day, Groundhog Day, Hawaiian Luau, Chinese New Year, Bastille Day, the Fourth of July, and the Cherry Blossom Festival. Teams researched their topics and presented written proposals in class. Upon approval of the topics, RSP and Village School student teams met with the elementary school teachers, the assistant principal, and RSP faculty members who coordinated the lists of art materials required for the construction of the hangings. RAP students used a heavy canvas and did most of their own art work. RSP and fifth and sixth graders used lighter muslin and were helped with their projects by the elementary teachers.

Logistics

At RAP, the curricular home for the project was COllaboratory, a full-year, six-credit course required of all RAP students. The curricular home at RSP was the Learning Community Laboratory, or Lab—a variable-credit (1–2) course that met in the faculty dining room of the cafeteria every other week on Thursdays, from 4:30 to 6:30 P.M., and included dinner, a ninety-minute activity, and a reflection paper (Romanoff, 2000).

The first meetings between students and faculty were at the end of January. Approximately eighty RAP students, along with the Iolani and Le Jardin students in Hawaii, chose teams. Likewise, approximately eighty RSP and Village School students chose teams of four to six. Students in Maine and Hawaii freely exchanged their ideas on the project by e-mail and by MOO. The work on the hangings began in February for an early April exhibit of the Maine project at the Portland Museum.

A collaboration of this magnitude meant that Watts and I would have to remain in constant contact through personal e-mail and the telephone. I would be nearing the end of my school day in Maine when she would be beginning hers in Hawaii. Likewise, our students and the participating class-room teachers and museum staff found that in order to chat with their new transcontinental colleagues they had to factor in the six-hour difference. Russell Scholars wishing to chat with RAP colleagues in Hawaii often had to wait until midnight to reach them after dinner. Some students were able to arrange conferences in Walden3 at mutually agreeable times. Many students, both at RSP and at the Village school, experienced difficulty getting online on Walden3, due to a host of technical incompatibilities at their respective schools. We ultimately designated a central computer at both Maine sites to allow students to access both Walden3 and the COllaboratory e-mail listserv.

Arranging time for the RSP students to work with the Village School students and their teachers was often quite challenging because of the infrequency of the Lab meetings. RSP students and the Village School students and faculty made considerable sacrifices in order to arrange time for them to work together. However, knowing that their colleagues in Hawaii were working toward their own deadlines spurred the Maine students on to complete their projects on schedule.

The Exhibits

In April, students, the faculty, and museum personnel at the Portland Museum of Art (PMA) mounted twenty hangings for the first installment of "Celebrations: Windows into Culture." RSP students invited their Hawaiian colleagues to visit the exhibit on the PMA Web site and to make comments. The exhibit hung for two weeks at PMA before traveling to Hawaii, where it hung for two months in the Bishop Museum, alongside the twenty hangings created by RAP. The University of Hawaii RAP students documented their exhibit opening on their Web site, and the Maine teams were able to see their own hangings exhibited in Honolulu and to enjoy the photos of the RAP students at the Bishop Museum.

In September, the entire RSP/RAP exhibit returned to the Portland Museum of Art for two months. RAP students were able to access the PMA Web site to see their works hanging in Portland alongside the RSP works. An adjacent computer room at PMA allowed museum-goers to visit the RAP and Bishop Museum Web sites while touring the entire exhibit. RSP and RAP students and their team partners freely exchanged comments on the COllaboratory listserv. The comments of the students and the public indicated a great sense of accomplishment on both an individual and a collective level. Students, faculty, parents, and interested citizens visited the museums and their Web sites. The local and regional media covered the exhibit and the PMA experienced record attendance for an art exhibit in its public galleries.

Conclusion

Two geographically and culturally distant land-based learning communities met online and emerged as a community of learners. What began as a conversation in cyberspace between two teacher-administrators in Maine and Hawaii evolved into a learning community of nearly two hundred students, teachers, and administrators who regarded their distant collaborators as colleagues. A modest proposal grew into an intercontinental learning phenomenon as a result of good teaching practices and the possibilities inherent in the use of technologies for distance education.

Distance education exists on the premise that technology and teaching will combine to provide an effective learning experience for the student. To that end, distance education is a potentially powerful teaching and learning vehicle when deployed through formats that capitalize on both traditional and innovative pedagogies and learning formats. Learning communities are effective formats for nurturing academic success and for fostering a sense of solidarity and well-being by reducing the distance between students, faculty members, and the courses that make up their curricula. The absence of an in-person, face-to-face classroom experience is less important than the presence of a learning experience that affirms the individual and the collective efforts of students and teachers. As much as the use of technology can expand the physical distance between teachers and learners, it can also serve to reduce that distance by enhancing the sense of community among students and teachers.

Implications

Distance learning, through conventional technology, can create and sustain learning communities among students and other global citizens separated by great geographical and cultural distances. These models can be employed across a wide range of subject areas and cultures, from business to diplomacy, to facilitate learning, tolerance, and better understanding of others and ourselves. Students in different parts of the country, indeed around the globe, can productively communicate and learn about each other and about themselves. The same technology with which students are familiar at home and from school computer activities is an available tool for reaching fellow learners anywhere that Internet service can access.

A distant colleague of mine, Margit Watts, observed that we have found that the same philosophical principals that guide our learning community movement to improve undergraduate education within the brick and mortar of our universities should also guide the decisions about our new cyberspace learning environments. Now we face the responsibility of disseminating our understanding of learning communities not only to other conventional land-based institutions but also into the world now known as distance education (Watts, 1998).

References

Astin, A. W. *What Matters in College.* San Francisco: Jossey-Bass, 1993.

Astin, A. W. "Involvement in Learning Revisited: Lessons We Have Learned." *Journal of College Student Development,* 1996, *41*(2), 123–133.

Cho, S. K., and Berg, Z. L. "Overcoming Barriers to Distance Training and Education." *United States Distance Learning Journal,* 2002, *16*(1), Jan. 31, 2002. [http://www.usdla.org/html/journal/JAN02_Issue/article01.html]. Access date: Jan. 10, 2002.

Gabelnick, F., McGregor, J., Matthews, R., and Smith, B. "Students in Learning Communities: Engaging with Self, Others, and the College Community." In F. Gabelnick, J. McGregor, R. Matthews, and B. Smith (eds.), *Learning Communities: Creating Connections Among Students, Faculty, and Disciplines.* New Directions for Teaching and Learning, no. 41. San Francisco: Jossey-Bass, 1990.

Johnson, J., and Romanoff, S. "Higher Education Residential Communities: What Are the Implications for Student Success?" *College Student Journal,* 1999, *33*(3), 385–399.

Levine, J. H., and Tompkins, D. "Making Learning Communities Work." *AAHE Bulletin,* 48(10), 3–6.

Meiklejohn, A. *The Experimental College.* New York: HarperCollins, 1932.

Parks, M., and Floyd, K. "Making Friends in Cyberspace." *Journal of Computer Mediated Communication,* 1996, *I,* 4. [http://jcmc.huji.ac.il/vol1/issue4/parks.html]. Access date: Jan. 21, 2002.

Romanoff, S. "The Learning Community Laboratory: A Context for Discovery." *Journal of College Student Development.* 2000, *41*(2), 245–247.

"Russell Scholars at USM." University of Southern Maine. [http://www.usm.maine.edu/~rscholar]. Access date: Jan. 15, 2002.

Shapiro, N., and Levine, J. *Creating Learning Communities.* San Francisco: Jossey-Bass, 1999.

Steiner, V. "What Is Distance Education?" 1995. [http://www.dlrn.org/library/dl/whatis.html]. Access date: Jan. 28, 2002.

Tinto, V., Goodsell-Love, A., and Russo, P. "Building Learning Communities for New College Students." *Liberal Education,* 1993, *79,* 17–21.

Tussman, J. *Experiment at Berkeley.* London: Oxford University Press, 1969.

University System of Maryland, Institute for Distance Education. "Overview: Models of Distance Education, a Conceptual Planning Tool." 1997. [http://www.umuc.edu/ide/modlmenu.html#1overview]. Access date: Jan. 29, 2002.

Watts, M. "Rainbow Advantage Program." University of Hawaii, 1998. [http://www.rap.hawaii.edu/rapprograms.html]. Access date: Jan. 15, 2002.

STEPHEN J. ROMANOFF *is director of the Russell Scholars Program and associate professor of interdisciplinary studies at the University of Southern Maine.*

By discussing service learning and describing an online course as an example, this chapter focuses on service learning as a method for taking the distance out of the educational experience.

7

Passion for Learning, Passion for Life

Margit Misangyi Watts

No one will argue about the significance of getting today's youth involved in meaningful ways in their own communities. However, many disagree about how much value this kind of activity has within the construct of an academic environment. This chapter explores the possibilities of community service as a breeding ground for both the enhancement of academic learning and the use of a catalyst for engagement and passion.

> If I can change one kid's life, I can change the future. (First-year student)

Students today are not necessarily disenchanted—a term used to describe the apathetic, disengaged youth of the so-called Generation X. Some folks have the notion that these students couldn't possibly be disenchanted, because to be so would imply that there was a time when they were indeed enchanted. Therefore, it has been suggested that this generation is *unenchanted* and that they have never been passionate about anything.

> There are not too many things these days that can put a smile on my face. Working with those children somehow fills this void. (First-year student)

This is not an indictment against a generation of youth who have been the subject of much discussion—perhaps maligned—and have yet to create a place for themselves in history. It is, however, a stunning thought for educators working with today's youth. Whether we look to the bleak economy, the instability of the environment, the fragmentation of countries around the world, the dissolution of families, or just to the streets of inner-city America, something has created a vacuum. It is obvious that our students are often disengaged—or unenchanted. This chapter is not aimed at

New Directions for Teaching and Learning, no. 94, Summer 2003 © Wiley Periodicals, Inc.

trying to sort out the answer to the question of why we find this lack of passion; instead, it looks at community service learning as a possible solution to help students bring passion back into their lives, as well as serving as a model that creates an academic environment for teaching and learning that transcends the classroom walls. It is possible to send the students out beyond the classroom to work and learn, using distance learning in unique and engaging ways.

> I have interacted.
> I have maintained a positive attitude.
> I have had fun.
> I have learned.
> I have contributed.
> I have helped.
> I have fed and nourished the minds and stomachs of some children in Waikiki.
> I have changed. (First-year student)

These words are in response to having spent a few months spent in a community service project, looking for an answer to the question What is the purpose of higher education? Jacques Barzun (1991) suggests that the task of higher education is to pass on the social, cultural, and political heritage to the next generation. A well-educated person is seen as someone open to new cultures, ideas, and technologies, as well as one who remains current through independent learning (Simpson and Frost, 1993). Johnetta Cole (1994) argues that a student's time in college is "a time of training, not only for a career, but for life" (p. 17).

If one of the missions of an institution of higher education is to foster learning, discovery, discussion, and the gathering of information about the world, shouldn't students spend time experiencing this world? Should time spent at the university be a time divorced from the wider community? Is it not part of the academic mission of a university to change students' orientation toward their community? There is general agreement that we want to develop thoughtful citizens who contribute time to their communities. And most of us understand that education is not a one-way affair, nor is it value-free. But how much are we willing to incorporate and integrate community service into the curriculum? How, why, and in what ways do we want our students to change throughout their undergraduate years? Boyer (1987) suggests that undergraduates today are "products of a society in which the call for individual gratification booms forth on every side while the claims of community are weak" (p. 83). Perhaps we need to help students see the relationship between what they learn and how they live. The new movement of integrating community service within the curriculum is attempting to bridge the gap between theory and practice. The call for service is both a call for practical experience to enhance learning and a reinforcement of moral and civic values inherent in serving others. There is the hope that something within a student's undergraduate experience will lead to the development of a more competent, more complete human being (Boyer, 1987).

How do we know this to be true? Well, first we make the student the center. But what does this mean? It means that we get to know our students. Our knowledge of who they are and where they are in their thinking and experiences helps us design activities that allow learning to begin. Coles (1993) understands the need to know our students: "Unwittingly I had been drawing conclusions based on a limited capacity to absorb and reflect upon what the children around me were seeing and saying and feeling, and I had missed a lot" (p. 24).

As Mary Catherine Bateson (1994) suggests, "to become open to multiple layers of vision is to be both practical and empathic" (p. 12). One mission of undergraduate education is to provide the kind of academic environment that encourages students to reach out and grasp new ideas, experiences, and meaning. Bateson (1994) finds that there are many ways of learning and that "by encountering and comparing more than one version of experience, [the] realities of self and world are relative, dependent on context and point of view. Because we live in a world of change and diversity, we are privileged to enter, if only peripherally, into a diversity of visions, and beyond that to include them in the range of responsible caring (p. 12).

It is possible that community service learning offers us the ability to go outside the classroom and learn about the "others," finding out about their lives, thoughts, and struggles, reflecting on what our presence might mean, and, finally, discovering who we are. The presence of the other is always helpful, whether in a negative or positive way, in questioning familiar things. Putting experiences together, yours and mine—side by side, allowing them to integrate and meld—this brings insight (Bateson, 1994).

> Doing this [service learning] really brought out a part of me that I didn't know was in me. (First-year student)

Suggesting community service within the context of the undergraduate experience is usually met with nods of approval; requiring it is controversial. Certainly, there is agreement that participation in community service is a win-win-win situation. The benefits to the community are enormous, especially when volunteers are sorely needed. The college or university benefits as its image improves within the community, and students benefit in myriad ways. Community service may be one of the "first truly meaningful acts in a young person's life" (Boyer, 1987, p. 213). These experiences have been proven to raise self-esteem, build character, empower students to see themselves as integral players within their communities, foster the development of lifelong commitments to their communities, and give them opportunities to become responsible, engaged adults. Coles (1993) finds that "a major consequence of community service for many, young and old alike, is an inclination to think about those words 'community' and 'service,' to seek in them some larger vision that might hold the attention of that community known as a nation and that institution dedicated to serving the people, known as government" (p. 280).

Coles further offers that there is a place for intellectual reflection within the scope of community service learning. Service itself is a challenge; there is no doubt about that. What is of concern to the wider academic community is whether service will engage students in intellectual pursuits. Will participation enhance and reflect the mission of higher education? Certainly, service creates a sense of usefulness and connectivity with the community. Is it also a means of putting to use what one has learned? Or, more important, does this experience augment the teaching and learning within the classroom? Coles (1993) wonders what changes take place in the mind as it "responds to courses taken and to events weathered through visits to soup kitchens, schools, nursing homes, and prisons" (p. 172).

In *Habits of the Heart* (Bellah and others, 1985), the authors are convinced that a "good society" in the end depends on the goodness of individuals. They find that individuals must become involved, that we all have a "debt to society," and that, ultimately, we are all interconnected; we are dependent on one another. If this is the case, then service can be viewed as a catalyst for social change.

> Helping this country, this planet, is no easy task, but it is one mission that I plan on completing. (First-year student)

And if one main mission of education is to encourage students to take with them a predisposition to learn, then learning in context should be viewed as a positive approach.

Many new learning theories have recently emerged, all attempting to pinpoint the most effective educational methods. However, all of them seem to agree that education truly requires students to be invested in the learning process, and that we do our best teaching and learning when we can apply knowledge and relate it to ourselves. This leads to deep and connected learning and appears to be an excellent way to foster the kind of academic environment that leads students to make meaning. Christensen, Gavin, and Sweet (1991) point out that all learning is contextual in at least three senses: new knowledge is acquired by extending and revising prior knowledge; new ideas acquire meaning when they are presented in a coherent relationship to one another; and knowledge becomes usable when it is acquired in situations that entail applications to concrete problem solving. These three meanings of context set a frame of reference for thinking about effective teaching" (p. xiv).

It is possible that "classroom instruction and community service combine synergistically to enhance learning" (Markus, Howard, and King, 1993, p. 418) and that this combination leads students to become personally invested in the process of learning. Students begin to take ownership of their education; they see the connection between service and learning.

In addition to understanding that connection, however, students must be given the opportunity to think about what they are doing. This reflection takes place where we actually sit between our own regular world and the world that we visit (Coles, 1993). It is in this reflection that the learning occurs, it is here that both teacher and student begin to understand the significance of community service experiences, and it is this kind of teaching and learning that takes the distance out of the educational experience.

Interdisciplinary Studies 291

> There are a lot of things you don't know about yourself until you give back to people who need things more than you. (First-year student)

At the University of Hawaii, a course—IS 291—is being used to give first-year students an opportunity to participate in service learning activities. The course is variable credit, and with the exception of a few workshops, it is totally online. Students register for the course and they are given information regarding two required workshops, paperwork that needs to be completed, and a Web site that has the remainder of pertinent information to begin the course.

For the course, students are advised that they must complete two hours weekly, working for an agency in the community. These agencies have been contacted beforehand and are prepared to work with college students. All of the information regarding the agencies and contact information is contained at the course Web site. Students also access the course syllabus, readings, evaluation forms, and other information regarding service learning on the course Web site.

To complete this course in a semester (for two credits), students must do seven things:

1. Complete liability waivers
2. Choose an agency, contact it, and arrange to do the service learning
3. Work for a community agency for at least two hours weekly
4. Send electronic journals to the course faculty weekly
5. Complete skill and learning evaluations (found at the Web site)
6. Complete the assigned reading
7. Write a final reflective paper

All of the information regarding these tasks is online and a faculty member and graduate assistant are available by e-mail at all times to help coordinate and expedite the necessary steps to get the service learning under way.

Instead of being an "add-on" to an existing course, IS 291 is a course that augments the other work being done by the students. Students are encouraged to choose an agency that might be dealing with issues of some relevance to other courses they are taking. For instance, perhaps working for a neighborhood board or the legislature would be of interest to a student taking political science. However, a student interested in sociology might be interested in working for the humane society or a social welfare agency. In this way, all of the work out in the community has connections to the work being done within the classroom. In addition, as the course stands alone and is managed quite easily through the use of the new communications technologies, students are empowered to connect theory to practice while earning their required credits.

Service learning can't always be a separate course, and it sometimes needs to fit into the context of traditional course design. As stated before, everyone thinks community service is a good idea. After all, there are few who can argue about the value of feeding children, nurturing the elderly, saving the environment, or helping the homeless. But it is difficult to convince many academics of the value of this kind of experience within the context of a college course. They ask many questions, such as, Is this "real" learning? Is it possible that we are watering down the content of this course to include a service project? or Given the limitations of a semester, shouldn't we be careful about how we spend our time? Yes, this is real learning. What is it that we are watering down? We should be *very* careful about how we spend our time. After all, this is the kind of learning that will make a difference. This will help college students "change." These experiences will indeed bring passion to their lives. Participation in meaningful community service will only serve to broaden their understanding of all the other learning throughout their undergraduate experience. This is how we foster the development of those concerned citizens, informed members of society, caring individuals who will make good decisions about the future.

Involvement in community service might actually raise the level of engagement of our students. It is apparent that many arguments can be made in favor of participation in a project, regardless of the degree of connectivity to the content of a particular course. After all, we want to build positive bonds between our students and the communities in which they live. We want to renew the belief that it might just be possible for ordinary citizens to have a hand in solving the problems of society. Meaningful experiences can be seen as inspiration for our students to view themselves in the greater context and to begin to act for the common good. They might even learn to value themselves and their contributions more highly. In the end, community service validates their whole college experience. They can't help but learn. And we can't help but allow this learning to flourish.

References

Barzun, J. *Begin Here: The Forgotten Conditions of Teaching and Learning.* Chicago: University of Chicago Press, 1991.

Bateson, M. C. *Peripheral Visions.* New York: HarperCollins, 1994.

Bellah, R. N., and others. *Habits of the Heart.* New York: HarperCollins, 1985.

Boyer, E. *College: The Undergraduate Experience in America.* New York: HarperCollins, 1987.

Christensen, C. R., Garvin, D. A., and Sweet, A. (eds.). *Education for Judgment.* Boston: Harvard Business School Press, 1991.

Cole, J. "A Marriage Made in Heaven: Community Colleges and Service Learning." *Community College Journal.* June/July 1994, 14–20.

Coles, R. *The Call of Service.* New York: Houghton Mifflin, 1993.

Markus, G. B., Howard, J.P.F., and King, D. C. "Integrating Community Service and Classroom Instruction Enhances Learning: Results from an Experiment." *Educational Evaluation and Policy Analysis,* 1993, 15(4), 410–419.

Simpson, R. D., and Frost, S. H. *Inside College: Undergraduate Education for the Future.* New York: Insight Books, 1993.

MARGIT MISANGYI WATTS is director of Rainbow Advantage/Freshman Seminars at the University of Hawaii at Manoa. She is active in the national movement for information literacy, is involved in campus initiatives in distance learning, and recently authored a text for first-year students, College: We Make the Road by Walking.

Interlude: A Conversation with Howard Rheingold, Founder of the Well, an Online Community

Margit Misangyi Watts

Howard Rheingold is widely known as both the editor of *The Millennium Whole Earth Catalog* (1994) and as one of the founders of the Well, an asynchronous online community. As an avid participant in this community, Rheingold began writing about his experiences. He addressed these experiences in two books: *Virtual Reality: The Revolutionary Technology of Computer-Generated Artificial Worlds* (1992) and *The Virtual Community: Homesteading on the Electronic Frontier* (1994, 2000).

A few years back, Rheingold was in Honolulu for a conference and I had the occasion to meet with him for a lengthy discussion about technology, virtual communities, and the future. Sitting high above Waikiki, overlooking the turquoise ocean, Rheingold talked at length about his experiences, hopes, and fears. I was initially interested in finding out about his definition of a good community, and I asked him to outline the criteria he might use. Rheingold was quick to reply with the following:

> I don't think that good community and bad community is so much a part of it. I think that the primary definition of it is that people have to put up with each other one way or the other, whether it is because they live together or because they are connected by some common belief, or they need to do business with each other. Or they are people who share an interest and have conversations and relationships that take place over time. There is a sort of idealization of community from the olden days that doesn't exist any longer. We also have a utopian notion that we can go back and create better ones, and this notion has been with us forever.

I had to ask whether his online community, the Well, fulfilled the notion of a great community. He said no and continued, saying,

> I'd say any place where people get to know each other well enough becomes less wonderful. The honeymoon is always over eventually and it's a mixed bag. The Well is now fifteen years old; it was only five or six years old when I began writing about it. People have been married, people have died. You communicate with the same people all day long, everyday, and some of them

become good friends and some of them become very irritating. It think that's true just about anyplace. I think that hearing about what happens to each other is what distinguishes a community from simply a collection of people exchanging information with one another. You either care about people or dislike them.

Understanding that he was suggesting a new way of thinking about the concept of community, I offered the possibility that perhaps we never really had the kind of community we like to idealize. He agreed readily:

I think that in one sense the world has changed and there are more people and more technology and more 'things' that are artificial. I mean, here we are, sitting in Waikiki. Certainly that must be true here. I grew up in the desert, and now living in San Francisco for a number of years I see there has been this mindless expansion of the material world. Now that it covers everything, we begin to see that we have lost something. However, I agree with you. I think that a lot of these small towns that people seem to yearn for were not very tolerant places for people who were different. And those are the people who went to cities, like San Francisco, to get away from that intolerance. So I think that people cared for each other, knew each other more intimately than they do in big impersonal cities, but they were just as judgmental and gossiping and bigoted as anywhere else.

We continued discussing the concept of community and he suggested that the German word for community—*Gemeinschaft*—and the German word for society—*Gesellschaft*—actually represent opposing ideas. He submitted that the community versus society could be translated into village life versus the city. He considered the differences between real and virtual communities by proposing that "what really connects you here to the United States of America is an idea. What connects you to people in the virtual community is geography, a kind of idea. The point being that we are always arguing about redefining what we mean by community and how it [has] changed."

Reminding him of his own experiences in the Well community and his new enterprise, Electric Minds, another type of online community, I asked him to explain his intentions with this new community. Rheingold explained that the purpose behind Electric Minds was to create a place accessible to millions of people to share ideas. He stated, "It was important to me to show that besides endless billboards of what you have to sell, or pictures of your family and dog, or whatever people want to publicize [on the Internet], this could be a place where people could communicate with each other. The idea was to simply demonstrate that this medium had room in it for social interaction and that people could have intelligent conversation that was relatively simple."

I wondered if his community was living up to his idea. He felt that it was indeed successful but recommended that we broaden our discussion to include other technologies. Rheingold advised, "When you talk about technology and community, I think you really have to go back to automobiles, railroads, jet planes, air conditioning, elevators, high rises, and the suburbs. These are the things that have accumulated over the last century that people have accepted as normal, because they give us freedom and power. Also, in retrospect, these things changed our lives not necessarily for the better, because in some ways we are now more alienated from the people we live with in our neighborhoods."

I then had to ask what comes next. If those kinds of communities aren't feasible because we are overpopulated and because technology slips in between us and the next person, perhaps in the form of an air conditioner that keeps the doors closed, where do we go from here? Rheingold maintained that only the really privileged and rich or the really poor way out in the countryside have the opportunity to experience less alienated communities. Observing that systems agriculture can't compete with agribusiness any longer, Rheingold supposed that the small farm communities were no longer working, that there are too many people and a solution to the problem is not in sight.

Perhaps we are moving into Kevin Kelly's "hive mentality," I suggested, and the new communication technologies are assisting us. Rheingold was disturbed by this notion and indicated that it was unpleasant to him.

> I am an American. Americans are very individualistic and have somewhat a different attitude towards the group than other [nationalities] do. The Japanese, Chinese, or Indian—or any place where there are a whole lot of people—they have to learn how to live with people, and it becomes somewhat of a different way of thinking. I think that it may be people who think in the old way [who are] never quite satisfied with the new ways. Socrates was concerned that if we wrote things down, it would make us forget things and therefore make us think differently. It believe that's true; we probably do think differently, since we read books and use radios, telephones, televisions, and computers. But maybe that is just the human thing: thinking in new ways in relation to new tools.

I agreed that change most often makes people uncomfortable, but Rheingold added, "You know, we got here because we embraced change. It is amazing that not too long ago—twenty or thirty thousand years ago, people went to Alaska and somehow found their way to the tip of South America. It is a new territory every year. Thus, you would think we had embraced change, but there have been long periods in which the idea of security, solidity, and tradition have been worshiped. So, change does bring fear."

Wondering if there was some sort of backlash occurring, I asked him to consider how often we relate the notion of family, home, and community back to Thoreau and nature and getting in touch with our humanity. I stressed that the neo-Luddites are concerned with technology and its prompting us to pre-fer trees in simulated 3D as opposed to the real ones out in the forest, full of sap and pine needles. I asked Rheingold if he thought that was the direction we were moving in. He replied by first admitting to be somewhat of a neo-Luddite himself, and then he anticipated that "we will have lost something. We don't have many forests any more. We have nice 3D representations of them, but they are not the same thing. We don't know how to possess that which created them and took a long time [bringing them] into being. Unfortunately, it is not going to take a long time for them to disappear."

We discussed "appropriate" technology and tried to discern how this might be defined. Rheingold referred to the technology of the seventies and pointed out that it was perhaps more intimate. An example he used was of small electrical plants that were possibly more appropriate for humane set-tings. Given his expressed concern over the future—of trees and otherwise, I asked him to predict it for me. Rheingold lamented,

> What do I predict? Well, there is a huge amount of money being spent and a great deal of knowledge circulating about how to manipulate people's per-ception of advertising. Technology is something to buy. It sustains this econ-omy that's been going on since the Second World War. It feeds on itself and makes this huge middle class live better than it did beforehand. Kids don't die, people are fed, they have a place to live, and at the same time we have a very large super-rich class and a very large number of people in the under-class, which keeps on growing. And the natural foundation for it all seems to be poisoned. So I don't think it is sustainable. I think some kind of cataclysm will result in the next twenty to forty years.

Surprised by this rather pessimistic view, I wondered what kind of cat-aclysm he could imagine. He was convinced that we were living in the midst of one already. With the salmon disappearing from the Columbia River and the extinction of the monk seal, he imagined a world more and more devoid of living things, and, as a result, less human.

I challenged his point of view by playing devil's advocate, insinuating that the natural evolution of things just happens to be that certain plants and animals are no longer necessary. He countered with some concern: "Aren't necessary for what? I think what you define [as being] *human* is what is really at stake. I mean, if we are defining [being] human in terms of artificial environments that our technology has created for us, that's one thing. [Technology] doesn't seem pleasant to me or [as] exciting as it used to be. It has homogenized the world in a way that makes me sad. The world is not as diverse, interesting, or complex, and we can't seem to find motives other than commercial ones. There has to be a change."

I speculated on what kind of change and then indicated how incon-gruous it was for him to display such neo-Luddite thinking when his name was almost synonymous with technology and virtual communities. I invited him to explain how he integrated these seemingly disparate aspects of his personality. He was glad to answer:

> I think there is a humane way to use the technology that might otherwise just be a crowded marketplace. Is it better to be online all day than to do other things? I don't think so. It is not an either/or situation. What is the appropriate use of tools? You have to ground that question in what is an appropriate way for people to spend their time. It ultimately comes down to the questions raised a thousand years ago about "a good life," a "good person," and why and how one [should] live. People have always had different ideas about those things. And it is the question about how to use technology that poses a philosophical question. We haven't been asking ourselves these more abstract questions as a society. We have been consuming the ideas and the products that have been sold to us. We have a great machine for marketing and selling products. In fact, virtual communities are one of the things you can use these computers for, but you can't sell it as a substitute for participation in a family, taking part in voting in an election, or living in your apartment.

Agreeing that we should be concerned about humans and their tools rather than tools and their humans, I asked him to address his concerns about this conflict. Rheingold conveyed his belief that television and movies and other packaged entertainment have reduced the discourse from what it should—or could—be. He asked,

> Is it black or is it white? Point—counterpoint? No shades of gray? It may not be that technology is either going to save us or be the source of all evil. It may come down to how we think about technology, how it ought to be designed or deployed. Who is given the power? Whom does it disempower? Whom does it enrich? And whom does it impoverish? And what can we do about that? I tend to think in shades of gray and want to take into account the complexities, because simple solutions don't necessarily work in a complex world.

Rheingold expresses concern that we have been cheated by the mass media, considering that this relatively small number of people (the media) have the means to determine how a large number of people perceive things. He maintained that television sensationalized the Internet and really didn't communicate the Internet's ability to offer everyone the opportunity to participate in a larger democratic discourse. Rheingold criticized the media for commercializing those aspects of the Internet—the commercials that show distant relatives making contact by phone, computer, or some new handheld gadget.

Rheingold's daughter was in the room with us, patiently awaiting the end of our conversation so that she could take off with her mother and father for a day at the beach. Her presence was the catalyst for my asking him what he would like to see in the future for his daughter. His answer took me somewhat by surprise: "I am afraid that the world she lives in and will live in is an artificial one, and I am glad that she is able to see some of the world as it is, without a thousand shopping centers and skyscrapers. Yesterday, we visited the botanical gardens. Of course, that is an artificial re-creation of what this whole place (Hawaii) used to be like, but at least we can get some sense of it."

Tongue in cheek, I suggested that earphones, goggles, and monitors were all we would need to experience everything in the future. He responded with a personal story: "You know, a few years ago I took my daughter out into the backyard to say 'this is a tree.' I told her that this was a 'real' tree, different from what she sees on the screen. And she looked at me with a 'dad!, what are you talking about?' look. I told her, 'Well, by the time you get to [be] my age, it is going to be very difficult to tell the difference, if there is a difference.'"

I could see he was upset with the possibility that technology might remove what we now consider to be real. And yet he is still amazed that we can talk to people who live on the other side of the world from us. However, he smiled, "Being able to talk to someone across town was frightening to our grandparents. Maybe they were right. I think we haven't really allowed ourselves to come to terms with what it all means."

We watched the ocean fifteen stories below us, lapping at the white sand, and we ended our discussion with the agreement that many more such conversations needed to occur.

8

Text immersion is a way to get at information literacy because students learn to use the tools of knowledge management—computers, networks, software, and critical thinking, which they have contextualized through their ordering of raw data into information.

The Shallow End of Cyberspace

Michael Bertsch

Educators should use text immersion to teach reading and writing because it is the best way in our dynamic culture to learn reading and writing. Students master the machines of information as a consequence of learning to read and write. Access to digitized information requires not only the ability to read but also the ability to manipulate the machines that display digital media. Thus, a newer literacy is born that encompasses reading, writing, and basic computer knowledge; information literacy follows text immersion. So when we talk about the shallow end of cyberspace, we must understand that "literacy" collects a fatter meaning, and text immersion classrooms fatten up student literacies beyond the written word. Text immersion nurtures pattern recognition by repetition and invention and discovery. Robust recognition ability allows quicker, farther-reaching discovery and an increased ability to see connections.

Text immersion works in the same way we learn to sing advertising jingles in the shower; in real life, we're surrounded by ads and their music, surrounded by the tunes of our culture, immersed in Western tonal music all our waking hours, and sometimes in our dreams, too. How? By moving through supermarkets, elevators, and dentists' offices, listening to the radio and TV, and by singing songs in church, around campfires, and at birthday parties. We live with music. We pick up the basic rules of harmony through our immersion in music. Through being immersed in the sounds of music in our daily lives, we can all follow along in our mental ears.

Immersion in some medium to learn *about* that medium is a very old concept. Stone Age humans practiced the apprenticeship tradition. Whether as a hunter or as a shaman, in cooking, in tanning, or in dancing, ancient peoples passed data, skills, and stories between generations using apprenticeships. Young apprentices were allowed to play with some of the raw

NEW DIRECTIONS FOR TEACHING AND LEARNING, no. 94, Summer 2003 © Wiley Periodicals, Inc.

materials of the craft, thereby developing a tactile relationship with the craft or skills, helping to develop a foundation for learning. Interestingly enough, the more we humans learn, the easier it is for us to continue learning, because our brains have an incredible facility for associative memory and pattern recognition. The more we learn, the more we *can* learn, and this knowledge about learning shows us the best way to educate our students about reading and writing: we ask them to read and write using modern tools under expert tutelage.

When we immerse very young students in active and valuable written communication, we open and reinforce the neural pathways in the brain that process language and reading and writing. We also open and reinforce the mechanical pathways associated with typing and machine use. Opening these brain routes early in a child's life exposes the child to the tools he or she will use to succeed throughout his or her life. Children are built to learn, and we can do great good for our culture by taking advantage of the tendencies built into our humanity—hardwired into our biological motherboards, so to speak. Once these pathways are open and responding, students can progress easily if teachers pay attention. Teachers in text immersion classrooms ask students to use technology in learning, which subsequently develops their fluency in telecommunications.

We teachers must adopt notions of these broader fluencies and literacies and invite students to begin swimming by creating activities that use collaboration and technologies in the construction of their own texts. For example, when working with young writers, we can develop an environment wherein writing is valuable and valued. We can have them write stories and then ask them to swap tales and talk about what worked and what didn't work in each story. Then we can have them revise the stories for better effect on word processors—playing with words. Finally, we can publish juried stories in a class newspaper and on the school's Web site, with students doing the computer graphics and text layouts. Schools can maximize benefits from this activity if other teachers formulate activities around reading the newspapers and developing responses.

We know that becoming educated takes a lot of work. And if students can't see immediate benefits from being educated, their motivation toward becoming educated diminishes. When we humans are quite young, we play with sounds, trying to imitate our parents. We eventually make meaning with these sounds to request maybe a glass of pear juice. Play is an important aspect of language learning in children, and aware teachers may exploit this human tendency to beneficial effect in the classroom. Thus, the play aspect associated with text immersion provides a respite from formal learning, and at the same time, it provides immediate benefits to the student for having learned. As students increase their skills base, the production of text becomes easier and pleasure in the tasks grows, yet learning continues to take place readily and easily. There are many reasons why this happens.

Teachers in text immersion classes focus on creativity, fluency, and correctness, paying attention to rules as a matter of being members of a particular discourse community. Children playing with sounds are aware of belonging to their limited discourse community and follow its rules, which helps explain why children do not grow up imitating, say, vacuum cleaner sounds. In English class, for example, the rules are well established, yet instead of requiring strict adherence to rules, text immersion gives permission to *use* language. To use language means to do something with it, and getting it done means the writing has to be accurate—eventually. Inaccurate writing yields unintended consequences. Unclear requests go unfulfilled. Accurate writing gets results. Exciting writing that is also accurate really gets attention. This is how we become members of particular discourse communities.

Exciting writing is neither boring nor repetitious. Writers immersed in text for class have to try new ways of writing things. In our speech, we have little sayings that we'll drop into conversations to keep things moving, but when the very same terms are typed and read over and over, they no longer carry meaning. "You know?" comes to mind. New expressions and techniques must be developed, learned, and nurtured. Text immersion classrooms provide real-life, full-contact language learning, and students clearly benefit from it. Their vocabularies increase along with their reading comprehension, their typing speed gets better, their ability to manipulate the machines improves, and they learn to piece together clear concepts from a wildly unusual variety of sources. Text immersion means that each student swims on his or her own with the rest of us. Each has to develop individual strategies based on individual values. This is an important skill and requires much practice. These classrooms function under rules understood and acquired only by participation in the making of meaning—both in writing and through reading. This is text immersion. Firefighters immerse themselves in their particular technologies in order to master them, as do doctors, shaved-ice vendors, teachers, and cheesecake bakers. So it should be with reading and writing. This immersion must involve play because play is experimentation. Firefighters balance axes, coil hoses, and stack ladders, bakers find that sour cream holds a decorative shape better when it's cold, teachers discover what works under which conditions by trying different things under different circumstances. Play is really work when we talk about learning.

Teachers must explicitly grant permission for students to play in text immersion classes because teachers control classrooms. Teachers must say that certain types of language play is both okay and beneficial, and the early granting of this permission is important. This may be done through extra-credit writing activities, where one point is awarded for every new word used to revise famous sentences, such as "It was a dark and stormy night." Students could add clauses for more points. In both face-to-face and virtual classes, teachers should let the examples become a bit silly; we're not seeking the perfectly euphonious sentence, though we may find it. We're teaching the process of playing with language. It is the machines that allow this to take place. As the coordinators of freewheeling wordplay sessions, we become closer to our students by virtue of our participation.

The best way to create opportunities to practice language play is to immerse students in the written language. The student must read and write constantly to participate in the class, practicing critical thinking while becoming fluent in the means of rendering thought into words. Chat rooms and other text-based environments, such as MOOs and RPGs (Role Playing Games), are excellent for this. Many advantages for both the student and the teacher emerge from text-based play, mostly having to do with the development of fluency in thinking, writing, and typing. But the most significant advantage demonstrated in these environments is the reduction of the distance between the teacher and the student through membership in the same discourse community under identical circumstances. Typographical errors plague all typists, and when teachers hammer out a funny gaffe, not only does everyone giggle, but, in that moment, the teacher somehow becomes more human, less to be feared, and therefore more effective in coaching about the making of meaning. Still, because teachers also model correct and varied writing, the teacher must maintain adherence to the rules of English, because, with the advent of text messaging on cell phones, a truncated form of abbreviated typing that is popular among students younger than twenty, teachers must require full, correct sentences. Consider the sentence "Dont let txt msgs creep N2 yur clas [sic]." We do not want to promote this type of spelling as formal writing, although informal writing does have its place and should be acknowledged; it, too, reinforces its own discourse community. But it does not have its place in the classroom, where we teach and model formal English literacy.

As children mature into a literate society, they must master fundamental written and verbal skills in order to participate. Speaking, reading, and writing are largely functions of the left brain, where data are ordered and where letters are decoded into words and then into concepts. One problem in our culture is the heavy influence of television. Thus, the holistic right side of the brain, which operates by pattern recognition, does most of the work of making meaning from television input. This leaves the analytical left side of the brain, which codes and decodes, terribly understimulated. After years of watching TV shows "about nothing," a generation of students have nothing to think with. A TV watcher's left brain languishes and is underused. It is possible that computers can combine the best of TV with the best of reading and writing, as well as combining the best of holistic thinking with the best of analytical thinking. Under skilled teaching leadership, text immersion classrooms can mix what is called the "lean back approach" of passive television viewing with the "lean forward approach" of computer use. The possibility is there for us to exploit, and text immersion is one approach to using the best of both media.

Computers make this type of learning possible, but using computers to process language requires two levels of literacy. A writer's ability to express clearly is tied to his or her fluency with the mechanisms of expressing his or her intended meaning—using such machines as computers, VCRs, scanners, printers, and audio and video editors, as well as using various methods and means of storage, transmittal, and display. Moreover, a reader's ability to decode texts from the Internet is tied to his or her ability to find and view those texts. Information-literate students must be able to locate, access, extract, and manipulate many different types of data forms.

A text immersion class could approach the challenge of information literacy through a project requiring the manipulation of various data forms. This class would employ a quick Web search to produce a site holding, for example, Super Bowl advertisements, viewed in streaming format. The class could convert these files to video for classroom use or for the school library. The students may select favorite ads and then develop on the class home page, or on the board, a public list of "elements" that make up the ads. The class could write papers saying why the ad is a favorite, based on how the elements work together, and they could also develop multimedia presentations illustrating these discoveries. TV ad analysis provides for thousands of activities, each activity rich in multiple media.

Flexibility is one great feature of the text immersion classroom. Before the advent of information technologies, the exercise previously mentioned could have been performed by using magazines, newspapers, pamphlets, and even labels on foods. Way back when—twenty years ago—the technologies for making and displaying text would have been used to help students learn to read and write. Nowadays, the technologies have changed, but the theories of immersion have not. Arrowhead chippers and hide tanners immersed themselves in their crafts and thereby learned. That we now use digitized media and immerse our students therein for purposes of learning follows the same theories of immersion: use it to learn about it.

Text immersion is as much about reading as it is about writing. Our reading vocabularies are always larger than our writing vocabularies, and we make sense out of what we are reading from what we've already read. Thus, the more we have read, the more new words we can understand, which in turn allows us to understand even more complex writings. Building a reading vocabulary is best begun when the reader is young. That's why educators have always urged parents to read to their young children.

One interesting side effect of using text immersion is the decentering of the teacher's role, placing the learner at the center, where she should be. That the teacher is valuable in the classroom is beyond question. However, the dynamic of power and control changes in a text immersion classroom because everyone's writing looks largely the same on the screen in ten-point type, causing ideas to be viewed as central—over and beyond who has provided the ideas. In order to exploit this feature, teachers must participate in a text immersion classroom. When teachers write a paper on the same topic they assign their students, they can expose to their students their drafting and writing processes, and this is the means by which the master teaches the apprentice; the learner must be shown *what* may be done, along with the *means* by which it may be done. Nonparticipating teachers do a disservice to their students, and their students don't learn anything new.

But the most significant consequence of teachers participating in text immersion classrooms with their students is that the traditional distance is reduced between the teacher and the student—the master and the apprentice. When everyone appears in 10 point Courier type, no one is taller or shorter, so to speak, than anyone else. When everyone posts rough drafts and then changes them, everyone is a writer and a reader, but the teacher serves as a model. In face-to-face classrooms, the change is most noticed when teachers write along with the class, which makes teachers more human somehow.

Teachers cement their membership in the discourse community through their participation in the text immersion classroom. Through this membership they demonstrate the value of the written (and read) word. It is the very act of participation that removes the distance between the students and the teacher, as everyone in a text immersion classroom is a member of the same discourse community. As in every community, we find varying skill levels.

The more we practice anything, the better we get; reading and writing is no exception. Practice strengthens the mental aspect of coding and decoding, as well as the physical aspect of making text—Kerouac's "writing and typing cramps" (1958, pp. 72–73). Practice under expert tutelage brings to mind Gary Snyder's "Axe Handles" (1983), in which he discusses a new handle that is carved using the axe on which it will be used; he states that "the pattern [for the handle] is not far off" (p. 5). In composition classes, we teach the writing process, and in text immersion classes, the instructor models the process. When we define *text* as any environment requiring interpretation—such as the text of a romantic relationship or the text of a film or play or political viewpoint—we enrich the definition of text immersion. The meaning of a word is its use in the common speech, so when we teach the written word, we also teach the awareness of context, because the meanings of words change over time; the word *gay* comes to mind. Thus, text immersion asks us to evaluate cultural contexts with respect to information literacy and the construction of meaning. When we dig deeply and ask our students to do the same, we reinforce their neural pathways, which students require for success in a rapidly changing world. We also reinforce those same pathways in ourselves, thus maintaining the robust intellectual life we educators cherish so strongly. These reinforced neural pathways are the inland waterways upon which critical thinking travels.

Writing as communication is different from talking; writing produces and requires one kind of language, whereas speech requires another. We have to understand that we're preparing our learners for entry into a space where they will have to read, think, and write quickly and accurately, a space at once both compelling and frightening. Success in this space requires superior information literacy, of necessity long in development, so it's best to enter this vast and deep pool of knowledge from the shallow end.

The swimmers at my high school saw above the pool door a sign saying, "Sweat in practice so you won't bleed in the game." Text immersion provides that metaphorical practice pool: it's safe, and there's coaching and clean towels. No one loses his job, gets demoted, or is ostracized because of a dangling modifier or a comma splice. It's a perfect environment for language learning because it is so safe.

We're preparing our young people to accept stewardship of the planet after we're gone, and students must be literate and fluent in the world of telecommunications to perform well there. One cannot innovate if one is not fluent in the medium. The world will adopt telecommunications technology not because it's better, which it might be, and not because it's faster, which it is. The world will adopt telecommunications technology because it's cheaper. Period. Once we accept this, we can move forward in a conscious way to prepare our students to enter the working world ready to succeed, not just survive. Language itself is the matrix upon which we hang our particular views of the universe, forming the subdirectories of our personal hard drives, the honeycombs of our inner hives, and the mail slots behind the front desk at our Hotel Cogito. Much more than an organizational tool, language is the music that plays the band we all joined, and text immersion classrooms are the best places to learn that language.

References

Kerouac, J. "The Essentials of Spontaneous Prose." *The Evergreen Review*, 1958, 5, 72–73.
Snyder, G. "Axe Handles." *Axe Handles*. San Francisco: North Point Press, 1983.

MICHAEL BERTSCH *has taught in the California Community College system for fourteen years and is a partner in BeLearning.com, a Distributed Learning Services provider.*

This chapter discusses the use of learning cells in classrooms.

9

Cyberphilosophy, Learning Cells, and Distance Education

Wesley Cooper

In the journal *Teaching Philosophy,* Monika Langer published an article (1985) about her experience and that of her colleagues at McGill University with the Learning Cell Technique. It addresses some of the problems encountered in large classes, especially in such disciplines as philosophy and other disciplines in the humanities, in which one-on-one or small-group give and take is a prized dimension of teaching and learning. She describes a rigid routine for introducing the qualities of a seminar into large undergraduate classes. Following a description of this routine, a few variants of Langer's technique are sketched.

To fix ideas, consider teaching to a large class in an undergraduate course called cyberphilosophy, a branch of a more traditional field called philosophy of technology. Like its parent, cyberphilosophy addresses factual questions (What is technology? What is a computer?) and normative questions (Ought we to welcome new technologies into our lives? Is participation in virtual communities psychologically or socially constructive?). On the factual side of cyberphilosophy is the question, Is the human body a technology? The received view on this question is, of course not. For one thing, to suppose so would seem to introduce God into the philosophy of technology, or at least a very powerful designer of this particular technology—the body. A technology surely implies that there is a technologist. But this is widely regarded, in these naturalistic and Darwinian days, as an unwarranted intrusion of theology. Moreover, the paradigm cases of technologies are *extensions* of the body, such as tools (screwdrivers) and weapons (rifles), to which we assign a function (driving screws, killing). So a good portable definition of technology might be: an extension of the body

NEW DIRECTIONS FOR TEACHING AND LEARNING, no. 94, Summer 2003 © Wiley Periodicals, Inc.

to which we assign a function. Now, although I *could* assign a function to my body (I hereby designate my body to be a paperweight to hold down items on this desk), and some societies have been known to regard some human bodies as living tools—as Aristotle did when he classified certain human beings as natural slaves, I won't have to fight to convince the reader that no human body per se has a naturally assigned function, Aristotle notwithstanding. To that extent, the existentialists were right in saying that "existence precedes essence." Within parameters set by morality, not to mention good taste, we are fated to choose what to do with our lives and our bodies, without the option to pass the buck to some external authority. (But we can choose to subordinate our lives, bodies, and choices to an external buck stopper, which is precisely one choice among many.)

A question on the normative side of cyberethics is, Do virtual communities serve any good purpose? The received view on this question is, it depends on the community. For the sake of argument, accept that this is basically correct. For instance, if two e-mail correspondents constitute a virtual community, or if many contributors to a Usenet newsgroup do so, then most people who know about e-mail and Usenet would answer the question affirmatively. So replace the original question with a sharper and less easy-to-answer version that relates to the use of computer laboratories.

Do discussions in an online virtual reality serve any good purpose? There may not be a received view on this question, because the technology of online virtual realities is still pretty esoteric, having been explored so far only by relatively small subcultures within the educational establishment. One view is this: asynchronous communication through e-mail (or MOO-mail and others) and mailing lists (or Yahoo groups and others) is an invaluable new tool in the teacher's toolbox. Synchronous "chat" is less valuable, but it has a role when it's not forced into a rigid class assignment structure, unfolding by serendipity at the students' initiative.

The Learning Cell Technique is prized by philosophers who want to share the subtle and rewarding pleasures of Socratic dialogue, which is arguably the best way to migrate into the world of ideas—and should be done despite the barrier of large classes in modern universities. If tutorials and small seminars are not a live option for today's philosophy professors, is there any way for them to approximate their value in a class of twenty to a hundred students? The traditional Socratic method of teaching becomes distorted when class size rises above seven or eight, because in larger classes some students inevitably fall out of the discussion, and a few are more likely to dominate the exchange with the professor.

The value to be approximated has to do with intellectual give and take and the background study that prepares the tutorial or seminar student for "the event" of the discussion itself. In a large class, it is too easy for students to attend without preparing themselves in any significant way, and to sit there without participating in any significant way causes students to disappear in the anonymity of the lecture hall. The Learning Cell Technique changes this. First, it requires that students bring some written work to class on the day of learning cell (LC) discussion. In fairness to other students who have done the preparation, and in order to ensure the quality of the discussion, this requirement should be enforced. The instructor can judge what writing assignment will be most appropriate, but I find that three or four questions and answers on the week's reading will usually keep the discussion humming for an hour. The questions should be brief and easy to understand, and they should address something in the reading that might be found puzzling, difficult, or unclear. Students are to prepare written answers to their questions, ideally saying something that solves the puzzle, assuages the difficulty, and removes the unclarity.

An example might be helpful: the class could be reading Kevin Kelly's book *Out of Control* (1995), and a student may be uneasy about Kelly's key concept of a vivisystem, articulating this unease by writing out the question Are living things to be classified as vivisystems, or do only life-like nonliving things qualify?

Next, the student attempts to remove the unease by answering the question, writing in a way that will challenge the opinions of the others in his or her learning cell.

Kelly's concept of a vivisystem (1995) is the concept of something whose constitution and behavior are governed by the principles that govern biology (the *bio-logic,* as opposed to the *clockwork logic* of traditional Industrial Age machines). He is particularly interested in what he calls artificial vivisystems, giving such examples as planetary telephone systems, computer virus incubators, robot prototypes, virtual reality worlds, synthetic animated characters, diverse artificial ecologies, and computer models of the whole Earth (p. 3). It seems logical that Kelly would recognize natural vivisystems as the complement to artificial ones, and that natural vivisystems would simply be all living things, since they all possess bio-logic. But he also writes elsewhere in the book as though vivisystem and living-thing-or-organism are mutually exclusive categories: "Scientists debate whether the evidence of self-correcting cohesion seen in the Earth's global geochemistry qualify Earth as a large organism (Gaia), or merely a large vivisystem" (p. 233). So it seems that organisms are paradigms of bio-logic that vivisystems approximate, rather than being vivisystems themselves.

You might want students to prepare answers that are briefer or longer, depending on the class and context. But the crucial thing is that students arrive at the LC discussion with prepared work. Then the instructor asks the students to gather in small groups, perhaps putting chairs in circles or in some such way, creating subgroups within the class. Groups of four are a good size, but teachers have had success with groups ranging from two or three to six or seven. After introductions, if the students haven't met, one of them volunteers to get things rolling and asks one of his or her questions. At this point, it is vital that the others in the group respond before the questioner reads or rehearses his or her answer; to read the answer directly is to forestall conversation. After each member of the group has had an opportunity to respond, the questioner can compare the others' responses with his or her prepared answer. And then the next person in the group repeats this process, until everyone has had an opportunity to raise a question for discussion. And then this process begins again, until questions are exhausted or the allotted class time ends. Meanwhile, the instructor may want to mingle with the various groups and have members of each group sign an attendance sheet. These sheets can be useful for checking whether students are mixing with others or not. Forming into different cells for different LC discussions is a good thing, maximizing the learning that comes from experiencing how other minds approach a problem.

At the end of the discussion, the instructor collects the LC exercises and marks them, perhaps commenting on them. Comments can be especially helpful for directing a student's attention to an area in which he or she has promising ideas that could be developed in a research paper. The Learning Cell Technique structures class time in such a way that Socratic dialogue is possible. The written assignment helps ensure that the conversation is well informed. The small groups, or *cells,* guarantee that everyone speaks, raises questions, and expresses thoughts.

Some instructors, in some contexts, may reasonably want to devote all the class time to LC discussion. However, a great deal of work was involved, because of all the marking and commenting. And in the final analysis, it may be that considerable class time should be set aside for both lectures, in which a sustained argument or point of view is presented, as well as student presentations, which develop important skills that are different from the Socratic ones. What should be emphasized is that the Learning Cell Technique is adaptable. Consider its adaptation to an Internet environment.

Through e-mail, Web pages, and educational virtual realities such as a MOO that I run on an Internet-connected server in my office, the students and their teacher are brought together in an expansive and continuous "electronic world" that complements, without replacing, the triweekly classroom meetings of the class; at any rate, that is the idea. It's not that the virtual classroom has replaced the physical one, at least in my experience. Rather, a complex hybrid has emerged with some unexpected features. For instance, replacement of the hard copy "paper" (a coolly utilitarian artifact, often ink-smeared and grubby) by its Web-published equivalent (forced into elegance by the rigors of HTML) has been entirely smooth and natural. The students enjoy constructing the pages and often fashion them into minor objets d'art, adding another dimension of delight to reading a good paper, although it is made perfectly clear that philosophical content determines marks, with HTML flourishes being *l'art pour l'art.*

The enhancements that cyberspace makes to the Learning Cell Technique are not, on balance, so great that the author would have his students migrate to the "electronic world" simply for improved learning cell discussions. For one thing, there are detriments as well as enhancements—notably the absence of face-to-face encounters and the difficulty of organizing the discussions. The absence of F2F is not a totally negative outcome of cyberspace interaction, as there is something to be said for the cerebral mind-to-mind communication that cyberspace facilitates. But on the whole, it comes out, in my view, as a negative when classroom time is available for LC discussions. The online version might be ventured as a novelty now and then, but normally there's not much point to them.

However, they could be an important resource for teachers who are relying on the pure model of distance education: online teaching without the traditional classroom. There are certain advantages to the online LC format. For instance, someone in a learning cell might have wanted to know more about the Gaia hypothesis when the point was made about vivisystems. If a MOO object had been linked to a Web page on the topic of Gaia, one could issue the command to display that object, and the browsers of everyone in the group would go to the Gaia page, facilitating a discussion of the Gaia hypothesis in a more informed way than would have been possible in the classroom. Instructors can send each group to a different virtual room, so that there is no background noise from other groups to distract them. And discussions can be recorded so that there is a permanent record. And so forth. Taking advantage of the virtual environment makes for much work, especially when compared with the always-available in-class format. However, a "pure" distance educator without responsibility for several classroom lectures/discussions each week might find that the work is manageable.

References

Kelly, K. *Out of Control: The New Biology of Machines, Social Systems and the Economic World*. Cambridge, Mass.: Perseus Publishing, 1995.
Langer, M. "The Learning Cell Technique." *Teaching Philosophy*. 1985, 8, 41–46.

Wesley Cooper is a professor of philosophy at the University of Alberta. He is the author, recently, of The Unity of William James's Thought.

Experience should come before book learning. Let's turn educational practice upside down and see if we can do a better job of teaching and learning.

Experiential Knowledge

David Wolsk

Yu got tuh go there tuh know there
—Z. Hurston

If you want knowledge, you must take part in the practice of changing reality. If you want to know the taste of the pear, you must change the pear by eating it yourself.
—Mao Tse-tung

Education is experience, and the basis of experience is self-reliance.
—T. H. White

The students are standing along the wall, eyes closed or blindfolded. The teacher is finishing the instructions: "Remember, no talking, and keep your eyes closed. I'll be leading each of you to a chair. When two of you are facing each other, with the block of clay on the tabletop between you, I'll place your four hands on the clay. You are to make something together—any-thing—from the clay, without talking or opening your eyes." Within ten to fifteen minutes, the teacher asks them to open their eyes. The teacher interrupts the buzz of talk and students looking around at other tables. "Okay, let's talk about this experience."

The follow-up discussion may continue for several classes. Often, this generates related class and individual projects that last for months. These may include such topics as two-person decision making, nonverbal communication, creativity, and emotions.

What characterizes these class discussions and the follow-up projects they engender is their link to a personally felt decision-making experience.

The benefit: long-term memory. After many years, I remember vividly several Four Hands on the Clay class sessions. Contrast this with the oft-told tale of students cramming for an exam and forgetting it all soon after.

Back in the late sixties, this exercise was part of my Unesco-sponsored international education project. I was part of the experiential education movement of that period and I felt pretty sure that we were the answer to the chalk and talk and textbook learning approach, with its teaching equals learning assumption. Now, some thirty years later, with the world a much different place, and my experiences with it providing some sobering lessons, I'd like to propose a widening of the perspective on experiential learning.

There's a whole world outside of the lecture hall, library, and computer screen that needs to be experienced as a learning laboratory. That experience needs to include exposure to the decision-making processes of all segments of society. Students can benefit from exploring the *contexts and impacts of actions*—from the plant and animal world up to the human—without forgetting the bigger geological, geographical, and historical frameworks. I contend that too much is lost by starting with textbooks and lectures. This chapter will try to support that perspective.

First, let's think about the brain. Champion athletes listen to today's experts in sports physiology, and it's easy to understand why. As the four-minute mile becomes routine and other jumping, swimming, bicycling, and speed skating records fall, the athletes, coaches, and fans get the evidence. The more we learn about muscles, circulation, and high-energy nutrition, within the context of each sport, the better we can apply this information to performance improvements.

It's time we were just as focused on our brains, even though we have no measure of the four-minute "learning mile" or the calculus marathon—from introductory to advanced. A critical aspect of neurophysiology is concerned with the way our sensory systems function. The phrase *information processing* encompasses a concept crucial for pedagogy. From our own experiences as we grow up—experience by experience, we individually assemble our personal classification systems that impose an order on our universe. What my brain did with gamelan music in Bali was different from how my wife's brain handled it, and my experience of the music was even further removed from that of the Balinese listeners. Each brain is a personal pattern maker.

Each brain is also a perceptual control device. That concept comes from William Powers, whose book *Behavior: The Control of Perception* (1973) put a reverse twist to stimulus-response psychology. We know what we want, and our actions seek to satisfy the want. The complex brain-body system operates thousands of thermostat-type feedback circuits, each with variable set points. We push the button to achieve a comfortable temperature, put food in our mouth to maintain a satiety level, switch channels to reduce boredom, and read this chapter to achieve wisdom. Something quite magical happens when we stop seeing ourselves as stimulus-response automatons and switch on to input controllers with a hierarchy of input needs. For one thing, it shatters the image of students taking the professor's words and sticking them into their brains. All together now!

What are the applications of these concepts to pedagogy? The message is that we tend to manage students and organize learning experiences backwards. The teacher supplies the stimuli; students respond. We ask students to read texts and memorize lots of facts and figures. Then, they can apply this book learning to real life, with a discussion of relevant issues as well as field trips. In this backward sequence, the book chapters and vocabulary lists frame the discussion and experiences. The academic version of this can be experienced by listening to an argument between a sociologist and a psychologist, each using a language and database the other only dimly processes.

Today's human world may be the result. Whether it's global warming, major oil spills along our coasts, mutated bacteria no longer fearing our drugs, the degradation of our clean water supplies, governments that function poorly, poverty and unemployment, or ethnic conflicts, we all have our long lists of indicators heading south (literally and figuratively). All these can be seen as symptoms of insufficient mental muscle, an inability of mankind to manage well, an outcome of faulty learning processes.

The experts talk of being saved by a knowledge-based economy. But their concepts of knowledge are somewhat limited by the current emphasis on the cost-effective glories of print/graphics delivered from the two-dimensional rectangular screen—now alive with sound and motion, interactive, and pushy. It may be worthwhile to tease apart the different types of learning and "knowledge" that may result. The most basic is language: words that we apply to objects, names we use for people, and the words that make up our personal classification schemes. None of this is really simple, since the processing of language by the brain is exceedingly complex (Fauconnier and Turner, 2002). This is the kind of learning derived from lectures, discussions, and the reading of text. Although books can contain high-level abstruse concepts and create emotional reactions from the novelists' skilled characterizations and plots, it does seem useful to distinguish the once-removed quality of text comprehension from other kinds of learning.

Another kind of learning is what characterizes the disciplines and academia. Each discipline becomes a self-contained structure for concepts and research data. Thus, much creative intellectual expertise is contained in brains that are overstuffed with research data that is generated by very narrow questions and experimental manipulations that seek to control all variables but the one in question.

For my last category of knowledge, I'll use the colloquial expression *street smarts*. This is knowledge with an attitude; it is context-, time-, place-, personality-, culture-, and sociopolitical system-laden knowledge. And it's what we seem to protect our learners from. The only place to get it is out on the streets (and behind closed doors)—the places where decisions are made, where all the action is. Claude Levi-Strauss (1966) writes about the "science of the concrete" and introduces the term "bricolage" to refer to the practical artisan (the bricoleur), who is able to adapt his set of tools to make almost anything (unlike the engineer, who designs specific tools for each task). It's the kind of knowledge gained from apprenticeships with parents, masters, and elders—the system that ran the learning world for eons.

Ken Richardson (2000) has expressed apprenticeship as a "system in which social organization provides the structures to which cognitive systems (and brains) must attune, but in such a way that an individual can reflect back upon those external systems and continuously restructure them. Human intelligence resides in this dialectical relation between cognition and culture" (p. 189).

What's the application of this to pedagogy? Is there a workable alternative? Can we stop asking students to read texts and memorize a lot of facts and figures? Can we stop asking them to apply this book learning to real life with a discussion of relevant issues and field trips? The research base is thoroughly covered in a recent volume edited by Bransford, Brown, and Cocking (2000): *How People Learn*.

Suppose we tried to shift from backwards to forwards. That would mean exposing students to real life first, and then letting them explore the related books, Internet, and print sources, and then finally putting it all together with discussions of concepts, meanings, perspectives, and relevance. It would also mean students getting analytical on their own terms, built up from their *own* experiential world of classifying reality and apportioning emotions. From the word *own* comes *ownership*. When mastering something new and beginning with one's own experience, there is a critical sense of ownership that surrounds the outcomes of the learning experience. I am quite sure that the expression *love for learning* is rooted in this personally felt framework. *Existentialism* also seems like an appropriate concept.

When learning takes place from personal contact with reality, especially if that contact includes actions, decision making, reflection, and writing, all of the variables are accessible. The myriad chain of causal relationships can be traced out and assembled into coherent pictures. For example, in assisting a bureaucrat, the apprentice learner can feel the effects of the personalities and management styles of the surrounding hierarchy—the boss, coworkers, and subordinates. The interaction of these factors with the actual decisions and actions taken by the bureaucrat—and then the feedback—provides a framework for the personal learning and understanding that underlies true competence.

There is a big overlap here with what Peter Reason and John Heron (1995) term "co-operative inquiry." Students would engage in cooperative inquiry in order to "understand their world, make sense of their life and develop new and creative ways of looking at things [and]—learn how to act to change things they may want to change and find out how to do things better" (pp. 122–142). The approach has been used in a variety of situations, such as that with medical practitioners researching holistic medicine, groups with health problems working together to take charge of their lives, or women exploring gender issues in their workplace. All of these share a common thread: linking learning to personal action. A typical textbook on government—covered chapter by chapter by the professor and studied (with an essay or multiple-choice exam in mind) by the eager student—provides none of this. Even worse, the students who get a good mark on the exam feel that they *KNOW*. But what they know is like a disembodied skeleton. It's a blessing that they will have forgotten most of it in a few years. The good teacher, knowing this, will try to provide some contact with reality. A bureaucrat visits the class or the class visits a session of parliament or watches a question and answer period on television. Then there are the daily newspapers and videos and simulation exercises—long lists of resources available to good teachers to supplement the textbook. All to be passively absorbed. So the teacher who knows this includes discussion groups and problem-solving exercises. Currently, Web sites and e-mail interest groups can add a whole dimension of immediacy and global reach.

The students who find this interesting will likely end up quite satisfied that they are becoming competent in the subject area. In most cases, though, I feel that it's the kind of competence that has brought this world to the state it is in today. Like lawyers, doctors, engineers, and teachers, bureaucrats have been trained to be good bureaucrats. The shift to working knowledge and street smarts is not easy.

Different sets of problems arise when a teacher implements what is being proposed here. Students in the Unesco project described previously, doing exercises like Four Hands on the Clay, would say, "That was fun and fascinating, but now let's get back to our regular class work." And when I would send students out to job sites to meet with working people, they would plead, "Please give us time to do the background reading so we won't feel like uneducated dummies asking stupid uninformed questions. We have no right to take up a professional's time unless we've done our homework."

What's missing from this picture are two crucial elements: (1) the learner's need to grasp some essentials about the workings of their own brains and (2) metacognition, or thinking about thinking, which also needs to be introduced and understood by students. If all of this is beginning to sound like impractical dreaming, I suggest you check out the thinking about thinking and problem-solving curriculum developed by Reuven Feuerstein (1980). It has been used successfully with students of all ages. Both students and teachers benefit from thinking about thinking and from exploring learning processes and problem-solving structures together.

Aside from one particular curriculum, the broader issue is the necessity of making transparent to teachers, administrators, students, parents, politicians, bureaucrats, and taxpayers the necessity for this massive shift from conventional academic subject matter and its attendant skill sets thinking. We don't need to choose between cyberspace and real space. We will all benefit from students who have been exposed to explorations of the varied and individualized nature of learning, including cyberspace, real space, books, the arts, and apprenticeships—all as individual or cooperative group experiences. Students need to comprehend and file away for continual use their personal take on what works best for them and the combination of learning modes relevant for the range of learning experiences they seek.

As difficult as such a change may be, the evidence is that it can start to become a self-fulfilling prophecy. Once students learn how to learn and can pursue learning as a means of seeking answers to their own questions, their enthusiasm and energy level are boundless. This is not the place for the details. Also, I assume that anyone who picks up a book like this to read is probably quite capable of writing his or her own scenarios.

The harder question is, how can entrenched interests be entranced? There are obvious reasons for the past failures of educational reform. If society is able to continue surviving by muddling through, and if technological progress and human competence triumphantly reverse the downward trends in crucial ecological indicators, then I doubt that the radical reversals proposed here will succeed. However, the ranks of the deeply worried do seem to be growing. With the tools afforded by the Information Superhighway, a rapidly growing reform group could design, carve out, and construct a real-life experiential/existential base for our knowledge building. Students and parents are waiting.

A lack of examples is not the problem. Educational history is full of postsecondary institutions that exposed their learners to real life. Denmark's Free Gymnasium and Traveling High School and the examples given by David Lempert in his book *Escape from the Ivory Tower* (1995) operate with similar assumptions. With working adults as part-time students, professors in America's inner-city universities, linked by the Coalition of Urban and Metropolitan Universities (http://www.metrouniversities.com), are using their students' experiences as grist for the discussion/reflection/conceptualization process. For many years, Evergreen College has been crossing disciplinary boundaries and sending students out to investigate the real world. There is much to learn from this and much to applaud.

An example of a less formal nature is worth considering: mothers raising their children. Their lengthy sequences of real-life learning provide mothers with competencies and a learning-by-doing temperament that is quite unique. In her book *Maternal Thinking,* Sara Ruddick (1989) explores this setting for thinking rooted in and shaped by the activities of maternal practice. Unfortunately, for every new good example, there are just as many new bad examples. With the higher proportion of secondary students entering postsecondary institutions, the first-year programs now include a heavy dose of remedial English taught in the same disembodied way as that which failed during the previous years. In their desperate search for achieving outcome standards, educational saviors totally avoid the crucial question Why have students lost their ability and enthusiasm for self-directed learning? Like the medicos flogging drugs to reduce symptoms, the educos flog standardized courses as prescriptions to cure low levels of factual knowledge and the so-called basic skills.

I'll conclude with a personal vision. Each student will have learned how to evaluate and implement ideas—organizationally, productively, creatively, educationally, environmentally, structurally/materially, healthfully, artistically, protectively/safely, financially, legally, and interculturally—with competence in marketing/merchandising, shopping, parenting, the media, and communications. Collectively, it's all the stuff one needs for making a positive contribution to one's family, community, and country—and, in the process, for feeling pretty good about one's self. As an extra-added attraction, when students are out in the real world of activities, decisions, and relationships, they, and those interacting with them, function as mentors and teachers. Cooperative inquiry becomes a way of life. I'll let you draw your own conclusions as to the impact this could have on our world.

References

Bransford, J., Brown, A. L., and Cocking, R. R. (eds.) *How People Learn: Brain, Mind, Experience, and School.* Washington, D.C.: National Academy Press, 2000.

Fauconnier, G., and Turner, M. *The Way We Think.* New York: Basic, 2002.

Feuerstein, R. *Instrumental Enrichment: An Intervention Program for Cognitive Modifiability.* Glenview, Ill.: Scott, Foresman, 1980.

Lempert, D. H. *Escape from the Ivory Tower: Student Adventures in Democratic Experiential Education.* San Francisco: Jossey-Bass, 1995.

Levi-Strauss, Claude. *The Savage Mind.* Chicago: University of Chicago Press, 1966.

Powers, W. T. *Behavior: The Control of Perception.* Hawthorne: N.Y.: Aldine de Gruyter, 1973.

Reason, P., and Heron, J. "Co-operative Inquiry (with John Heron)." In R. Harre, J. Smith, and L. Van Langenhove (eds.), *Rethinking Methods in Psychology.* London: Sage, 1995.

Richardson, K. *The Making of Intelligence.* New York: Columbia University Press, 2000.

Ruddick, S. *Maternal Thinking: Toward a Politics of Peace.* Boston: Beacon Press, 1989.

Wolsk, D. *An Experience-Centred Curriculum: Exercises in Perception, Communication and Action.* Paris: Unesco, 1975.

DAVID WOLSK *has applied his postgraduate training in psychology, sociology, and neurophysiology to research, teaching, project administration, and consultation. As a consultant, he has developed and directed teacher training programs for education agencies in North America, Europe, and Africa.*

11

This concluding chapter articulates the philosophical dilemmas we face as a culture and how these must be dealt with in light of our educational models.

Taking the Distance out of Education

Margit Misangyi Watts

We shall never be able to separate ourselves from our own inventions, and to try to do so is perhaps only a step backwards in an evolutionary sense. Technology, after all, is an extension of the human mind, and we are creating new technologies that are extensions of tools we have crafted for years. Be it better spears for warfare or a new discovery about genetic imprints, we continue to move from simple to complex tools. However, we often find ourselves on fast-forward, forgetting to redefine our communities, our relationship to nature, and other perennial philosophical issues that are given a new twist by the emergence of computer technology and all its intricacies.

In the midst of what appears to be a fast track toward the integration of computer technology into our lives, some of us are in a feverish rush to use them in—as well as substitute them for—traditional educational environments. Others eschew the whole notion of computer technology transforming educational practice and attempt to avoid or ignore its influence on the way we live our lives. However, educational philosophy (*paideia*), perhaps for those of us infected with Eurocentrism at birth, is not some Platonic ideal edifice that transcends merely temporal events. It is very much a part of the culture that articulates, embodies, or professes faith in it. And any major change in that culture is going to force a change in educational philosophy, and, consequently, practice.

Technology has typically heralded new eras of economic growth and a corresponding improvement in the human condition. When we express anxiety about that vision, wondering if it is even more problematic than it seems, we're assured that there is nothing to worry about. Such a position ignores technology's locus in contemporary social, economic, and political contexts. Although it is clear that technology offers a venue through which we can address student particularities and extend access to increased numbers of students, distance education is often promoted as a cost-cutting solution to education's budgetary woes. Actually, it is often more expensive than traditional educational venues. And so we shouldn't build it just because we can.

One of the problems with encouraging administrators in higher education to take a more cautious view of the promise of technology is the historic equation of technology with progress. In our minds, progress has always been "good" and aligned with the concept of a better life. Nevertheless, the new computer technologies are not the panacea for students who want to know *if this is going to be on the test.* Viewed as such a solution, it will become obsolete once the entertainment value wears off. So whom are we serving when we look at distance education options? And why does it appear that some people are willing to give up much of what we know to be an intrinsically sound teaching practice for the lure of a model that is often "one to many." After all, isn't it interesting that many universities around the country are transforming their undergraduate programs to personalize the academic experience, yet, simultaneously, they are developing online courses that aim to disseminate information quickly, efficiently, and not necessarily personally?

Addressing the challenges facing higher education and understanding what place the new computer technologies might have in and out of the classroom are the first steps toward bridging the gap. In addition, educational philosophy must engage a philosophy of technology, which we hope will lead us to meaningful, relevant, and empowering educational practices. If used appropriately and grounded in sound pedagogy, computer technologies can enable us to create good models that have a wide impact. If we use technologies "just because we can," or for purely economic reasons, we might fail to meet the goals of engaging students by inviting them to help shape their academic environment.

An Educated Person

Schneider (1998) states,

> One of the things you learn from a liberal education is that context is everything. The new providers of distance education may be dramatically expanding the opportunities for "as needed" learning in a knowledge-based society. Or they may be trading on one of the most destructive myths of our time, the idea that intellectual powers, deep understanding, and valuable skills can be transmitted via delivery systems. Are the new models built on earlier learning? Or are educators putting online a "lecture-and-listen" model that never worked for most students in the first place? We know students of the new providers are getting credit hours; are they getting an education? [p. 11]

What, exactly, is an education? The mandate for institutions of higher education is to turn out educated citizens. The imperative is to help build stronger and more vital forms of community, develop an informed and involved citizenry, graduate people who can assume leadership roles, provide a competent and adaptable workforce, and foster environments in which students can develop their talents to the fullest. For some, the undergraduate experience should develop competent citizens who can communicate effectively, think critically, make informed judgments, and be concerned human beings. Others view the educational experience as a place for skill building and helping students view their education as a commodity that can be traded for a better life—most often in employment terms. In the midst of these two perspectives, the question that often arises is, what is an educated person? Part of the answer, surely, is that there is no single answer—there must be a whole host of answers, just as there is diversity among us in our natural endowments and world views. This idea challenges tradition in ways that create cracks in ageless educational foundations. The notion of diversity among students as well as among learning styles opens the door to new constructs. Certainly, computer technology has widened our choices for delivery, content, access, and practice, and it might be viewed as a tool to adequately address this diversity. There has been a great deal of national debate about higher education not meeting the needs of students or their communities. Basic skills are lacking and students graduate from college without developing them or appreciating the ability and joy of continuing with learning lifelong, let alone understanding their responsibility for and accountability to the communities in which they live. The report of the Wingspread Group on Higher Education suggests that there are at least three issues of concern to all universities across the nation. The three fundamental issues are (1) taking values seriously, (2) putting student learning first, and (3) creating a nation of learners. The challenges universities face are both how to address these issues and what effects they have on practice.

Much of what is awry in education is mirrored in society in general. Our culture has been partially disabled by the fragmentation within both the workplace and the family, as well as the alienation of people from each other and from the institutions with which they interact. In the university setting, the distance between students and the faculty is often vast, especially in larger institutions. For example, it is a shame that any senior at a university would not have a close enough relationship with a professor to warrant the writing of a letter of recommendation. But this is often the case and does not begin to address what the lack of interpersonal involvement has withheld from the students intellectually.

In addition, the almost universal fragmentation of the core, or general education, requirements of a university has made it virtually impossible for students to step back and see the value and strength inherent in a liberal education. Taking introductory psychology at 8:30 Monday morning means leaving that discipline behind at 9:30, until the next class, later in the week. Often, professors do not wish to see their job description include the weaving of their discipline into other disciplines, let alone into the fabric of our larger society. It is not surprising, therefore, that students are frequently incapable of making connections between what they learn in college and the rest of their lives. In fact, this is what is actually exciting about technology—not the access it affords to increased amounts of information (often out of context) but, rather, the access it gives students to an epistemological system, which allows them to generate knowledge by connecting seemingly discrete pieces of information.

Universities are also facing a restructuring of traditional educational paradigms. Regardless of what tools are being used, faculty and students are being asked to become actively involved in the transformation. Faculty members are challenged to broaden their role as educators. They must become more than transmitters of knowledge; they must also become facilitators of learning. Students, in turn, must reconsider their perception of education. They can no longer see themselves as receptacles of knowledge; they must become accountable for their own learning. In many respects, students today have already made the change; it is the arenas of higher education that are behind.

Proof of some of the problems of higher education comes with the alarmingly high rates of student attrition across the nation. A. Bartlett Giamatti (1985) suggests that "a liberal education rests on the supposition that our humanity is enriched by the pursuit of learning for its own sake; it is dedicated to the proposition that growth in thought, and in the power to think, increases the pleasure, breadth and value of life" (p. 121).

Giamatti (1985) implies that the university is the real world and that students should not be wary of learning for its own sake. However, in today's universities, students desperately cling to the hope that a college education will give them a ticket to a better future, which, in their view, means employment possibilities. If we continue to neglect the importance of enabling students to make connections across the curriculum and to their lives, we fail miserably in our mission to educate. We have actually undermined our own ability to foster the intellectual engagement that is at the foundation of higher learning.

We need to create common ground for valuing and accepting diversity, as well as designing a palate of educational experiences to serve a culturally rich population. This common ground should help students acquire a breadth and depth of knowledge and communication and critical thinking skills. Places of higher learning should allow students to become acquainted with methods of inquiry, examine personal values and social mores, foster an awareness of other cultures, gain self-knowledge, and achieve lasting intellectual and cultural interests.

The Distance *in* Education

Perhaps the Web and other Internet technologies can help us create learning environments that not only are constructivist in nature but also enhance our relationship to students. We would be on the right path if the development of online educational environments were created to help students make connections with information, with each other, with the faculty, and with both local and global communities. However, for the overwhelming majority of users, computers and related technologies are merely tools for accomplishing tasks. Knowledge has been reframed as an accessible, marketable public good. However, in so doing, one has to wonder if we are losing our best practices of teaching in the clamor for technological bells and whistles?

One of the practices that should be questioned in contemporary education is the current craze for imposing what is essentially a business paradigm on the academy. Not only have we confused people and products, we have also confused what education *is* with what it *does*. What it is is a process, and methods that zero in on outcome/product do little to measure process. What it does, we hope, is provide the means for students to continue to learn. Can we do this by adding distance to our educational practice? Or, more important, are we including those means in our practice of distance education? We are already looking for new learning environments—technologically enhanced or not, and we look to these vibrant academic arenas as the answer to students not engaged in learning. We don't need to reinterpret our educational philosophies, we need to rediscover or resurrect them. How do we promote these new electronic methods without also contributing to the demise of what we hold sacred in our educational practice? Why do we look to technology for renewal? As Americans, we have a mechanistic interpretation of the universe. We look to gadgets to solve our problems. We even question our creations no end. But we don't question what we should in fact create. There is no doubt that education at a distance is often worthy and marketable, an equalizer for opportunities and well conceived. But it is frightening to imagine higher education becoming a mass-market distribution system—one to many.

Taking the Distance *out*

In their book *When Hope and Fear Collide*, Arthur Levine and Jeanette Cureton (1998) suggest that we have "a generation that is indeed wearied by the enormous pressures they face economically, politically, socially, and psychologically. At the same time, they are energized by a desire to enjoy the good life and make their corner of the world a better place. This is a generation in which hope and fear are colliding" (p. 17).

And when hope and fear collide, students are often immobilized and appear passionless and unenchanted with the world around them. This is what we often view as apathy and lack of motivation. It is against this backdrop that universities are struggling to present a liberal education as a viable, significant, and worthy course of study. Colleges are restructuring their core requirements, retraining the faculty in active teaching and learning models, developing clusters of enriched programs designed to lure students to their campuses. One can see a move toward personalizing college campuses as an attempt to raise the retention rate and secure more students. At the same time, universities are jumping on the bandwagon of distance education as though it will solve their population dilemma, forgetting, sometimes, that in the hurry to get on board, they might leave behind solid pedagogy.

Presently, there are myriad online learning environments, some no different from the correspondence courses we had years ago, and others quite innovative in their approach to working with students. For example, the University of Phoenix (UP) has created a large niche for itself and it uses online conferencing software to facilitate learning. Its consumers are usually adult learners—those who have been in the workforce and are looking to augment their lives with an education. There is an emphasis in UP's program to communicate with the students often so that an academic relationship can be established. Conversely, there are initiatives that attempt to deliver education in a manner that services many students with only a few faculty members and many Web sites.

We should keep in mind the problems we are facing in our universities today and develop solutions to these that can be used in both face-to-face and online environments. If we continue to discover our best teaching practices, augment them in whatever manner necessary, and then bring good practice to any academic venue in which we operate, the delivery of our education will be sound.

In the beginning, computers became tools that everyone had to have. Schools across the country bought full labs, received equipment grants, and installed them into their schools. Somehow, there was an unwritten understanding that having a computer lab would relieve the other pressures and problems that schools were facing. Funny thing, though—it didn't work out that way. Tools are tools, and just that. And unless we use them to do our bidding, and don't allow ourselves to be driven by the possibilities until we understand what those actually are, we should tread carefully.

We have distance education going on around us all the time, be it the professor at the lectern in front of four hundred students or the Web site with pretty pictures and fill-in-the-blank quizzes on the Internet. Neither model approaches students as anything other than receptacles of information. This is not how to motivate them to engage in lifelong learning. In fact, all of the research on the problems within higher education seem to converge on one point, which is that more focus needs to be on the individual. Howard Gardner's work on multiple intelligences (1983) certainly heralded a new era of teaching practices, which focused on the special abilities of each student. The late Ernest Boyer (1987) conducted nationwide research to discover that universities needed to be more user-friendly, to borrow an overused term. Neil Postman (1995) suggests that we need a driving narrative to build a successful educational model. Parker Palmer (1998) agrees with Postman and strongly recommends that teachers become more in tune with their students. Their research suggests that we develop teaching and learning environments that are conducive to interaction between students and the faculty, creating educational strategies that support communities of learners. And, most recently, Richard Light (2001) highlights nine insights derived from his ten-year study of college students. Students reported that learning outside the classroom was most important, and they liked highly structured courses, preferred to work in teams, thrived on being given the challenge of their own projects, enjoyed the diversity found on a college campus, wanted interaction with teachers, hoped to learn how to write well, demanded good academic advising, and were enthusiastic about language classes (Light, 2001).

Do we integrate the findings of all this research as we develop our new online learning environments? Or are we blinded by the economic possibilities of extending educational options to students at a distance? It isn't an either/or scenario. The new computer technologies are often incredible when used to supplement face-to-face classes; they can also be dynamic in purely online venues. However, the beauty of these new tools is in the connections, flexibility, and additional communication opportunities they offer, not the availability that reaches many students at any cost—the greatest cost being sound educational practice. Be it a mimeograph, a typewritten handout, a desktop published syllabus, or a set of Web pages, it is all flat information. The most important component of what we offer is not the information but the context in which it might be delivered and practiced. The key is still a relationship between teachers and learners. This is not to say that reaching many students, offering each of them possibilities, and creating alternative ways of becoming educated are not noble courses of action. They are. But only if we keep the "distance" out, no matter what the venue.

References

Boyer, E. *College: The Undergraduate Experience in America.* New York: HarperCollins, 1987.

Giamatti, A. B. *A Free and Ordered Space: The Real World of the University.* New York: Norton, 1985.

Gardner, H. *Frames of Mind: The Theory of Multiple Intelligences.* New York: Basic Books, 1983.

Levine, A., and Cureton, J. S. *When Hope and Fear Collide: A Portrait of Today's College Student.* San Francisco: Jossey-Bass, 1998.

Light, R. J. *Making the Most of College: Students Speak Their Minds.* Cambridge, Mass.: Harvard University Press, 2001.

Palmer, P. *The Courage to Teach: Exploring the Inner Landscape of a Teacher's Life.* San Francisco: Jossey-Bass, 1998.

Postman, N. *The End of Education: Redefining the Value of School.* New York: Knopf, 1995.

Schneider, C. G. *American Association of Higher Education Bulletin.* Vol. 50, No. 9, May 1998.

MARGIT MISANGYI WATTS *is director of Rainbow Advantage/Freshman Seminars at the University of Hawaii at Manoa. She is active in the national movement for information literacy, is involved in campus initiatives in distance learning, and recently wrote a text for first-year students,* College: We Make the Road by Walking.

BIBLIOGRAPHY

Barell, J. *Teaching for Thoughtfulness.* New York: Longman, 1991.

Barlow, J. "It's a Poor Workman Who Blames His Tools." *Wired.* Special Edition: Dec. 1995. [http://www.wired.com/wired/scenarios/workman.html].

Barthes, R. *Elements of Semiology* (J. Cape, trans.). Boston: Beacon Press, 1967.

Barzun, J. *Begin Here: The Forgotten Conditions of Teaching and Learning.* Chicago: University of Chicago Press, 1991.

Bateson, M. C. *Peripheral Visions.* New York: HarperCollins, 1994.

Bellah, R. N., and others. *Habits of the Heart.* New York: Harper & Row, 1985.

Berge, Z. L. (ed.). *Computer-Mediated Communications and the Online Classroom.* 3 vols. Creskill, N.J.: Hampton Press, 1995.

Boyer, E. *College: The Undergraduate Experience in America.* New York: Harper & Row, 1987.

Boyle, H. C. "Community Service and Civic Education." *Phi Delta Kappan,* June 1991, pp. 765–767.

Brady, M. *What's Worth Teaching?* New York: State University of New York Press, 1989.

Christensen, C. R., Garvin, D. A., and Sweet, A. (eds.). *Education for Judgment.* Boston: Harvard Business School Press, 1991.

Cole, J. "A Marriage Made in Heaven: Community Colleges and Service Learning." *Community College Journal,* June/July 1994, pp. 14–20.

Coles, R. *The Call of Service.* Boston: Houghton Mifflin, 1993.

Cooper, W. "Walden Pond Moo." *Computing and Network Services,* 1995, 8(2), 6–8.

Crump, E., and Carbone, N. *English Online: A Student's Guide to the Internet and World Wide Web.* Boston: Houghton Mifflin, 1997.

DeWitt-Elmer, P. "Bards of the Internet: If E-mail Represents the Renaissance of Prose, Why Is So Much of It So Awful?" *Time,* July 4, 1994, pp. 66–67.

Fulwiler, T. (ed.). *The Journal Book.* Portsmouth, N.H.: Boynton/Cook, 1987.

Fulwiler, T. *College Writing: A Personal Approach to Academic Writing.* Portsmouth, N.H.: Boynton/Cook, 1991.

Gardner, H. *Frames of Mind.* New York: Basic Books, 1983.

Goodlad, J. *Educational Renewal.* San Francisco: Jossey-Bass, 1994.

Hartman, K., and others. "Patterns of Social Interaction and Learning to Write: Some Effects of Network Technologies." In Z. L. Berge (ed.), *Computer-Mediated Communications and the Online Classroom.* Creskill, N.J.: Hampton Press, 1995, 47–78.

Hawisher, G., and Moran, C. "Electronic Mail and the Writing Instructor." *College English,* 1993, 55, 627–643.

Horowitz, R. B., and Barchilon, M. G. "Stylistic Guidelines for E-mail." *IEEE Transactions on Professional Communications,* 1994, 37, 207–212.

Kaye, C. B. "Essentials for Successful Community Service Programs." *Educational Digest,* 1989, 55, 57–60.

Kearsley, G. "Explorations in Learning & Instruction: The Theory into Practice Database." [http://www.gwu.edu/~tip/index.html].

Kelly, K. *Out of Control.* Reading, Mass.: Addison-Wesley, 1994.

Lowry, M., Koneman, P., and Osman-Jouchoux, R. "Electronic Discussion Groups: Using E-mails as an Instructional Strategy." *Techtrends,* 1994, 39(2), 22–24.

Markus, G. B., Howard, J.P.F., and King, D. C. "Integrating Community Service and Classroom Instruction Enhances Learning: Results from an Experiment." *Educational Evaluation and Policy Analysis,* 1993, 15(4), 410–419.

McPherson, K., and Nebgen, M. K. "Connections: Community Service and School Reform Recommendations." *Education and Urban Society*, 1991, 23(3), 326–334.

"Minimalism (J. Carroll)." 1994, 1997. [http://www.gwu.edu/~tip/carroll.html].

Myers, E. L. "Open to Suggestion: Using E-mail with Developmental College Students." *Journal of Reading*, 1995, 38, 666–667.

Perelman, L. J. *School's Out*. New York: Avon, 1992.

Perry, T. S. "E-mail at Work." *IEEE Spectrum*, 1992, 29(10), 24–28.

Pomata, F. C. "Beyond Reading, Writing and Arithmetic." *The Journal of Experiential Education*, 1994, 17(2), 26–29.

Postman, N. *The End of Education*. New York: Knopf, 1995.

Sanders, B. *A is for Ox*. New York: Vintage Books, 1995.

Serow, R. C., Ciechalski, J., and Daye, C. "Students as Volunteers: Personal Competence, Social Diversity, and Participation in Community Service." *Urban Education*, 1990, 25(1), 157–168.

Serow, R. C. "Volunteering and Values: An Analysis of Students' Participation in Community Service." *Journal of Research and Development in Education*, 1990, 23(4), 198–203.

Simpson, R. D., and Frost, S. H. *Inside College: Undergraduate Education for the Future.* New York: Insight Books, 1993.

Sizer, T. R. *Horace's School*. Boston: Houghton Mifflin, 1992.

Smith, F. *Understanding Reading*. (3rd ed.) Hillsdale, N.J.: Erlbaum, 1986.

Spinuzzi, C. "A Different Kind of Forum: Rethinking Rhetorical Strategies for Electronic Text Media." *IEEE Transactions on Professional Communications*, 1994, 37, 213–217.

Sproull, L., and Kiesler, S. "Reducing Social Context Cues: Electronic Mail in Organizational Communication." *Management Science*, 1986, 32, 1492–1511.

Theus, K. T. "Campus-Based Community Service: New Populism or 'Smoke and Mirrors'?" *Change*, 1988, 20(5), 26–38.

Tillyer, D. A. "World Peace and Natural Writing Through E-mail." *Collegiate Microcomputer*, 1993, 11(2), 67–69.

Toffler, A., and Toffler, H. *Creating a New Civilization*. Kansas City, Mo.: Universal Press Syndicate, 1995.

INDEX

Alberta MOO, 46, 47
American Libraries, 23
Annual Conference on Distance Teaching and Learning (1999), 30
Apprenticeship, 92
Artificial vivisystems, 85
Astin, A. W., 51
"Ax Handles" (Snyder), 80

Barzun, J., 62
Bateson, M. C., 63
Bellah, R. N., 64
Berg, Z. L., 51
Bertsch, M., 10, 75, 81
Bio-logic, 85
Bishop Museum (Honolulu), 52, 57
Blackboard (software), 1, 42
Boyer, E., 62, 63
Bransford, J., 92
Brain as perceptual control device, 90–91
Brown, A. L., 92

"Celebrations: Windows Into Culture" (traveling art exhibit), 52, 56, 57
Chickering, A. W., 6
Cho, S. K., 51
Christensen, C. R., 64
Co-operative inquiry, 92–93
Coalition of Urban and Metropolitan Universities, 94
Cocking, R. R., 92
Cole, J., 62
Coles, R., 63, 64, 65
COllaboratory (RAP), 54, 56, 57
Community: defined as sharing interests/relationships, 9–10; definition of learning, 53; library defined as, 26–27; mandate for higher education to build stronger, 99; Rheingold interview on meaning of, 69–74; society vs., 70; technology impact on, 9–10; virtual, 34, 69–74, 84
Community service learning: benefits to students, 63–64; Course 291 (University of Hawaii), 65–67; to engage students in learning, 61–65; intellectual reflection element within, 64; as

opportunity to learn about "others," 63. *See also* Learning
Community-based education, 32
Computer technology: debate over educational use of, 34–35; used in higher education teaching, 39–40; library use of, 25–27. *See also* Technology
Control of Perception (Powers), 90
Cooper, W., 9, 11, 45, 49, 83
Course 291 (University of Hawaii), 65–67
Courseware, 42–43
Crystal, D., 14
Cureton, J., 101
Cyberethics, 84
Cyberlibrary, 25–26
Cyberphilosophy, 83–84

Day, M., 15
Denmark's Free Gymnasium and Traveling High School, 94
Distance learning education: computer technology as tool in, 39–40; concerns regarding teacher-student relationship in, 51–52; courseware for, 42–43; Either/Or critique of, 47, 48; exploring new technologies for use in, 40–41; integration of traditional and, 46–49; learning to teach in, 41–42; range of technologies/possibilities of, 1–2; reframing education/learning through, 100–101; reframing to take "distance" out of, 101–103; RSP-RAP collaboration in, 55–58

Education: challenges of restructuring paradigms of, 100; Computer technology as tool in higher, 39–40; controversy over using technology in, 97–98; debate over computer use in, 34–35; design process/opportunities of, 27–28; fragmentation of core/general requirements of, 99–100; inability to respond quickly to change, 38; inadequate funding of, 38–40; integration of distance learning and tra-ditional, 46–49; IT (integrative technology)-mediated, 46–47, 48, 49;

Back Issue/Subscription Order Form

Copy or detach and send to:

Jossey-Bass, A Wiley Company, 989 Market Street, San Francisco CA 94103-1741

Call or fax toll-free: Phone 888-378-2537 6:30AM – 3PM PST; Fax 888-481-2665

Back Issues: Please send me the following issues at $27 each
(Important: please include ISBN number with your order.)

_____

_____

_____

$ _____   Total for single issues

$ _____   SHIPPING CHARGES: SURFACE   Domestic Canadian
First Item $5.00 $6.00
Each Add'l Item $3.00 $1.50
For next-day and second-day delivery rates, call the number listed above.

Subscriptions   Please __ start __ renew my subscription to *New Directions for Teaching and Learning* for the year 2__ at the following rate:

U.S.	__ Individual $70	__ Institutional $145
Canada	__ Individual $70	__ Institutional $185
All Others	__ Individual $94	__ Institutional $219
Online Subscription		__ Institutional $145

**For more information about online subscriptions visit
www.interscience.wiley.com**

$ _____   Total single issues and subscriptions (Add appropriate sales tax for your state for single issue orders. No sales tax for U.S. subscriptions. Canadian residents, add GST for subscriptions and single issues.)

__Payment enclosed (U.S. check or money order only)
__VISA __ MC __ AmEx __ #_____ Exp. Date _____

Signature _____ Day Phone _____
__ Bill Me (U.S. institutional orders only. Purchase order required.)

Purchase order # _____
Federal Tax ID13559302   GST 89102 8052

Name _____

Address _____

_____

Phone _____ E-mail _____

For more information about Jossey-Bass, visit our Web site at www.josseybass.com

PROMOTION CODE ND03

TL89 Applying the Science of Learning to University Teaching and Beyond
Diane F. Halpern, Milton D. Hakel
Seeks to build on empirically validated learning activities to enhance what and how much is learned and how well and how long it is remembered. Demonstrates that the movement for a real science of learning—the application of scientific principles to the study of learning—has taken hold both under the controlled conditions of the laboratory and in the messy real-world settings where most of us go about the business of teaching and learning.
ISBN: 0-7879-5791-7

TL88 Fresh Approaches to the Evaluation of Teaching
Christopher Knapper, Patricia Cranton
Describes a number of alternative approaches, including interpretive and critical evaluation, use of teaching portfolios and teaching awards, performance indicators and learning outcomes, technology-mediated evaluation systems, and the role of teacher accreditation and teaching scholarship in instructional evaluation.
ISBN: 0-7879-5789-5

TL87 Techniques and Strategies for Interpreting Student Evaluations
Karron G. Lewis
Focuses on all phases of the student rating process—from data-gathering methods to presentation of results. Topics include methods of encouraging meaningful evaluations, mid-semester feedback, uses of quality teams and focus groups, and creating questions that target individual faculty needs and interest.
ISBN: 0-7879-5789-5

TL86 Scholarship Revisited: Perspectives on the Scholarship of Teaching
Carolin Kreber
Presents the outcomes of a Delphi Study conducted by an international panel of academics working in faculty evaluation scholarship and postsecondary teaching and learning. Identifies the important components of scholarship of teaching, defines its characteristics and outcomes, and explores its most pressing issues.
ISBN: 0-7879-5447-0

TL85 Beyond Teaching to Mentoring
Alice G. Reinarz, Eric R. White
Offers guidelines to optimizing student learning through classroom activities as well as peer, faculty, and professional mentoring. Addresses mentoring techniques in technical training, undergraduate business, science, and liberal arts studies, health professions, international study, and interdisciplinary work.
ISBN: 0-7879-5617-1

TL84 Principles of Effective Teaching in the Online Classroom
Renée E. Weiss, Dave S. Knowlton, Bruce W. Speck
Discusses structuring the online course, utilizing resources from the World Wide Web and using other electronic tools and technology to enhance classroom efficiency. Addresses challenges unique to the online classroom community, including successful communication strategies, performance evaluation, academic integrity, and accessibility for disabled students.
ISBN: 0-7879-5615-5

TL77   Promoting Civility: A Teaching Challenge
Steven M. Richardson
Offers strategies for promoting civil discourse and resolving conflict when it
arises—both in the classroom and in the campus community at large.
Recommends effective responses to disruptive classroom behavior and
techniques for encouraging open, respectful discussion of sensitive topics.
ISBN: 0-7879-4277-4

TL76   The Impact of Technology on Faculty Development, Life, and Work
Kay Herr Gillespie
Describes ways to enhance faculty members' technological literacy, suggests
an approach to instructional design that incorporates the possibilities of
today's technologies, and examines how the online community offers an
expansion of professional relationships and activities.
ISBN: 0-7879-4280-4

TL75   Classroom Assessment and Research: An Update on Uses, Approaches,
and Research Findings
Thomas Angelo
Illustrates how classroom assessment techniques (CATs) enhance both
student learning and the scholarship of teaching. Demonstrates how CATs
can promote good teamwork in students, help institutions answer the call
for program accountability, and guide new teachers in developing their
teaching philosophies.
ISBN: 0-7879-9885-0

TL74   Changing the Way We Grade Student Performance: Classroom
Assessment and the New Learning Paradigm
Rebecca S. Anderson, Bruce W. Speck
Offers alternative approaches to assessing student performance that are rooted
in the belief that students should be active rather than passive learners.
Explains how to use each assessment measure presented, including developing
criteria, integrating peer and self-assessment, and assigning grades.
ISBN: 0-7879-4278-2

TL73   Academic Service Learning: A Pedagogy of Action and Reflection
Robert A. Rhoads, Jeffrey P. F. Howard
Presents an academic conception of service learning, described as "a
pedagogical model that intentionally integrates academic learning and
relevant community service." Describes successful programs, and discusses
issues that faculty and administrators must consider as they incorporate
service learning into courses and curricula.
ISBN: 0-7879-4276-6

TL72   Universal Challenges in Faculty Work: Fresh Perspectives from Around
the World
Patricia Cranton
Educators from around the world describe issues they face in their teaching
practice. National differences are put into the context of universal themes,
including responding to demands for social development and reacting to
influences by government policies and financial constraints.
ISBN: 0-7879-3961-7

NEW DIRECTIONS FOR TEACHING AND LEARNING IS NOW AVAILABLE ONLINE AT WILEY INTERSCIENCE

What is Wiley InterScience?

Wiley InterScience is the dynamic online content service from John Wiley & Sons delivering the full text of over 300 leading scientific, technical, medical, and professional journals, plus major reference works, the acclaimed Current Protocols laboratory manuals, and even the full text of select Wiley print books online.

What are some special features of Wiley InterScience?

Wiley Interscience Alerts is a service that delivers table of contents via e-mail for any journal available on Wiley InterScience as soon as a new issue is published online.
EarlyView is Wiley's exclusive service presenting individual articles online as soon as they are ready, even before the release of the compiled print issue. These articles are complete, peer-reviewed, and citable.
CrossRef is the innovative multi-publisher reference linking system enabling readers to move seamlessly from a reference in a journal article to the cited publication, typically located on a different server and published by a different publisher.

How can I access Wiley InterScience?

Visit http://www.interscience.wiley.com.

Guest Users can browse Wiley InterScience for unrestricted access to journal tables of contents and article abstracts, or use the powerful search engine.
Registered Users are provided with a *Personal Home Page* to store and manage customized alerts, searches, and links to favorite journals and articles. Additionally, Registered Users can view free online sample issues and preview selected material from major reference works.
Licensed Customers are entitled to access full-text journal articles in PDF, with select journals also offering full-text HTML.

How do I become an Authorized User?

Authorized Users are individuals authorized by a paying Customer to have access to the journals in Wiley InterScience. For example, a university that subscribes to Wiley journals is considered to be the Customer. Faculty, staff and students authorized by the university to have access to those journals in Wiley InterScience are Authorized Users. Users should contact their library for information on which Wiley journals they have access to in Wiley InterScience.

ASK YOUR INSTITUTION ABOUT WILEY INTERSCIENCE TODAY!